I0584765

LOBATO

Follow the journey of one family throughout history

Christine D. Lobato-Ross

Copyright © 2021 by Old World Press

All rights reserved. No part of this book may
be reproduced or used in any manner without
written permission of the copyright owner
except for the use of quotations in a book
review. For more information, email:

Publishing@OldWorldPress.com

First paperback edition December 2021

Book design by Christine D. Lobato-Ross

Edited by Demetrius R. Ross

ISBN 978-0-578-34692-2

Contents

Preface

The journey of tracing my Lobato ancestors began after I took a DNA test with Ancestry.com. The results of my test indicated that I am 50% (Spain/Basque/Portugal), 36% (Native American), 6% (Jewish), and 8% (Other European). My family has been in Colorado for hundreds of years, so I began to question how I had such a large amount of European DNA.

While tracing my family history, I discovered that both Spain and Portugal were both awarding citizenship to anyone who could prove that their ancestors were driven out of Spain or Portugal during the Spanish Inquisition. After discovering that the Lobato name was on the Jewish Inquisition List, I chose to prove my Jewish heritage and apply for citizenship in Portugal. I was eventually granted my Sephardic Certificate of Recognition by the Jewish Federation of New Mexico and The Jewish Community of Oporto in Portugal. This certificate from Portugal must be obtained before applying for citizenship with the Government of Portugal. I am now a dual citizen of the United States of America and Portugal.

Proof in the form of legal documents or published written evidence had to be submitted with my family history to prove my family lineage. I began by tracking down the few men with the Lobato name that traveled to America in the 1500s. At that time, the Spanish Crown allowed Jewish Converts to travel to America to help in its conquest, but that ended as soon as it was reported that these men continued to practice their Jewish faith in the New World.

After I located the men who traveled to America in the 1500s, I documented their journey as well as their descendants until I discovered which one was my direct ancestor. I discovered many amazing historical events, but I also discovered many acts committed by my ancestors that I am not proud of or agree with. Regardless, this history is a part of my family history, and it is documented in this journey that eventually leads to me.

My ancestors were warriors, explorers, and conquerors who participated in many wars and conquests. They were awarded land and Indigenous Natives who were used for labor after they conquered them in America. Also, records were located of my ancestors who owned African slaves that they used as collateral to obtain loans. The slavery of Indigenous natives directly affects me because I am also an Indigenous Native American from the Pueblo Indian Tribe of Taos, New Mexico. I am also a descendant of an African American Slave. There are also many accounts of how my ancestors' provided funds, horses, time, and provisions to the natives. They also advocated for their fair treatment and married into many native families. Many hardships occurred throughout history, but it didn't prevent them from participating in them instead of going back to Spain or Portugal where they were being prosecuted or forced to convert from the Jewish faith.

Preserving the "Lobato" surname for hundreds of years over thousands of miles was a divine act that required many miracles. This historical journey begins with the first documented record of my family name "Lobato".

On my wedding day, my dad expressed how happy he was that he was gaining a son but sad that I was losing his last name of Lobato. His name meant everything to him, so I kept it. He raised us to be honored of being a Lobato, so I dedicate this book to him.

Introduction
The Lobato Name

A family name gives a group of people an identity that helps them preserve who they are and where they come from. Some of these names originate from symbols. In the bible, the twelve tribes of Abraham were identified using symbolic names of animals. For example, the Tribe of Benjamin used the symbol of the wolf to identify themselves. Their identity was described in Jacob's blessing:

> "*Benjamin is a **wolf** that raveneth; in the morning he shall devour the prey, at evening he shall divide the spoil.*" (Genesis 49.27) [1]

The Tribe of Benjamin's also used the image of the wolf on their flag. Many who originated from the tribe of Benjamin also adapted the name "wolf" into their family name in order to preserve their identity throughout history.

> "*In Spanish, **Lobato** means little wolf, which was often used as an equivalent of the Hebrew name Ze'ev, which is the traditional 'kinnui' ("secular equivalent") of Benjamin*" (Genesis 49.27). [2]

(Picture courtesy of the work of Jerusalem Heichal Shlomo door Benjamin Tribe, Author Utilisateur: Djampa)

(Picture courtesy of Israel-a-history-of.com)

The earliest record of the Lobato name was found in Galicia, Spain in an ancient book, "*Becerro de Castilla*", a Heraldic and Genealogical Encyclopedia written by Garcia Garrafa. This book dates back to **200 A.D.**, the time of Claudia Lupavia, the Visigoth Germanic Queen of Galicia. Heraldic researchers found evidence of a powerful family of Lobato Caballeros *(Knights)* who lived in Melon, Spain which is in Ribadavia *(Orense)* in Galicia. This is the place where all of the Caballeros of the Lobato name descend from. They supported the King and the Holy Church in the battles against the Moors, who swept over the Spanish Peninsula in **711 A.D.** [3]

Basco Lobato

Basco Lobato, lord of this house in Galicia, migrated to Portugal where he contributed to the founding of the monastery of Santo Domingo de Viana de Limia. [4] The Lobato family shield includes: A field of red, with three golden castles, placed in a triangle, and stitched edge of red, with seven wolves of their color. The Lobato Caballeros proved their nobility in the Orders of Santiago, Calatrava, Alcántara, Montesa, and Saint John of Jerusalem *(orders created to fight against the Moors, to aid with the Reconquista, and to aid in ensuring order by protecting pilgrims and helpless people).* They also proved their nobility in the Royal Chancery of Valladolid and Granada in the Royal Company of Marine Guards and the Royal Audience of Oviedo. [5]

The lineage of the Lobato family that connects Basco Lobato to the next descendant was found in a book that contains a description of the "Armas" *(shield)* belonging to the Lobato Family whose military letters of arms are registered in Portugal. They are organized and referenced according to a genealogical heraldic archive. The description of the Lobato Family Shield in this book is as follows:

*"LOBATO – A family from Galicia that originates from **Dom Vasco (Basco) Lobato** whose name comes from "Lobo", lord of the "Couto de Medon (Melon)" who migrated to Portugal. All with the name Lobato in Portugal have descended from him. The Lobato lineage has been preserved and now in the Quinta de Alvor, a part of Almade, and in the villas of Valladares and Monção, and in S. Mamede de Lisboa. There is a grave and a mass sung every year for **Pedro Annes (Eanes) Lobato,** to whom the king D. João I made nobleman. The shield letters are; in a red field there are three castles of silver surrounded by a border of gold with eight wolves of black, and one of the wolves is rising from the top of the middle tower of the castle."* [6]

Pedro Eanes Lobato

Pedro Eanes Lobato was born in Santarem, Portugal, and was part of King Pedro I's court. His name is signed on the instrument of witnesses that Pedro II published in Coimbra in 1360, which was used to prove the truth of his marriage to Ines de Castro. [7]

PEDRO EANNES LOBATO
(Desenhado sobre o que apparece nos *Retratos e Elogios de Varões e Donas)*

(Picture is from the Illustration by Alfredo Roque Gameiro in the book História de Portugal, popular e ilustrada, by Manuel Pinheiro Chagas)

Around 1367, Pedro Eanes Lobato was appointed as the vassal of Joao Afonso Telo de Meneses, Count of Barcelos and brother of Queen Leonor Teles. In 1384, Pedro Eanes Lobato participated in the siege of Lisbon, Portugal in which he gave tribute to John I, son of King Pedro I and half-brother of King Ferdinand. John I was also the Grand Master of Avis *(a military order similar to the Order of the Knights Templars)*. Pedro Eanes Lobato also belonged to the Order of Avis in Santarem. Pedro Eanes Lobato was knighted by John I, Master of Avis himself before the battle of Aljubarrota.[7]

In 1383, King Ferdinand of Portugal died with no son to inherit the throne. Princess Beatrice, daughter of Queen Leonor Teles was his only child. King Ferdinand promised her to King John I of Castile *(Spain)* and the crown of Portugal would belong to their heirs. The nobility and wealthy merchants of Portugal refused to support the claim of the princess, so Portugal remained without a king from 1383 to 1385. In 1385, the council of Portugal declared John I, Master of Avis, King of Portugal. After King John I of Castile married Princess Beatrice, he invaded Portugal to remove King John I, Master of Avis from the throne of Portugal. This was known as the battle of Aljubarrota.[8]

Portugal defeated Castile in the battle of Aljubarrota as well as many others. Pedro Eanes Lobato was part of the Council of war in Portugal that was led by Nuno Alvares Pereira. Pedro Eanes Lobato distinguished himself against the Castilian invasions and was rewarded with a Military Coat of Arms. Nuno Alvares Pereira also rewarded Pedro Eanes Lobato the rights to the village of Almada and Quinta de Cheira-Ventos in Amora. King John I of Portugal rewarded Pedro Eanes Lobato by nominating him as overseer of the Treasury and governor of the Civil House which was confirmed by Duarte who still designates Pedro Eanes Lobato as member of the King's Council. [9]

In 1415, Pedro Eanes Lobato could not help but to be part of the expedition to conquer Ceuta by being captain of one of the ships. [10] Ceuta is on the north coast of Africa on the Spanish mainland by the Strait of Gibraltar between the Atlantic Ocean and Mediterranean Sea, which is an important military and commercial chokepoint. [11]

(Picture is of the Caravela de armada of João Serrão. 1502)

King John I of Portugal made his son, Prince Henry the Navigator, Governor of Algarve which is located on southern region of Portugal. Henry the Navigator set up his shipping ports in Algarve and began to explore the coast of Africa after the conquest of Ceuta. He developed the caravel which could sail further and faster than any other ship. With the caravel, Portuguese mariners were able to explore rivers, shallow waters as well as open oceans that made Portugal the leader in exploration.

Prince Henry the Navigator also became the Grand Master of the Military Order of Christ, the Portuguese successor to the Knights Templars, that funded his ambitious plans of exploration. After receiving a world map from his brother Peter, Henry the Navigator created the "*Estudio General*" that united all of the sciences. His brother, King Edward, awarded him the profits from the trading of the areas that he discovered as well as the right to grant expeditions beyond Cape Bojador, an African coast. In Algarve, he held a monopoly on fishing and built a school for navigators and map makers. Prince Henry the Navigator also sponsored voyages, collecting 20% tax on the profits of naval expeditions. These trade routes made Portugal rich. Vasco da Gama was one of these explorers who was known as the first European to reach India by sea. Vasco da Gama was named Governor of India in 1498. Vasco de Gama also belonged to the Military Order of Christ. [12]

A stamp printed in Portugal shows Captain Francisco Lobato Faria and the sea god Neptune in the discovery of a sea route from Europe to India by Vasco da Gama [13]

Before Vasco da Gama became Governor of India, he accused Duarte de Menezes of corruption in a letter that he sent to King John III entitled "*Articles for the investigation of D. Duarte, Captain of India*". This letter contained accusations against the governor that are to be investigated as well as questions that should be asked of potential witnesses. One of these witnesses listed was **Jeronimo Lobato**. These witnesses were all men who were either related to or were like family to Vasco da Gama. [14] This record ties Vasco da Gama to Jeronimo Lobato. Vasco de Gama is tied to Henry the Navigator who is tied to Pedro Eanes Lobato. These allegiances ultimately tie Jeronimo Lobato to Pedro Eanes Lobato. Also, as documented, all of those with the Lobato name in Portugal descend from Basco Lobato as indicated in the Lobato Coat of Arms.

Jeronimo Lobato

Since the entire southern border of Portugal belonged to Henry the Navigator and his heirs, other ship owners and sea experts had to acquire ports in southern Spain mostly in Huelva and Palos De La Frontera. They had to also live in Spain in order to join the expeditions to America.

Jeronimo Lobato lived in Huelva, a neighbor of Palos De La Frontera. He was a very close personal friend of Christopher Columbus as indicated in the following referenced book:

A book was located that compiles information from documents found in the civil and ecclesiastical public archives as well as the government archives of Spain. It traces the journey and life of Christopher Columbus that began with the day he embarked on his first journey to the new world. This footprint of events was traced then shared with the Spanish Government. The journey of the writer of the book began with the writer sitting and writing on the same table where Christopher Columbus sat with the Prior, the doctor of Palos, Garcia Hernandez, the pilot Alonso Yáñez Pinzón, and his affectionate friend, Jerónimo Lobato. The writer also rested in the house of Jerónimo Lobato, the same place where Columbus rested. It was also documented that Jeronimo Lobato, and Christopher Columbus were "compadres". [15] In Portugal, a compadre is the Godfather of your son.

This book places Jeronimo Lobato in Huelva, Spain, a neighbor of Palos de La Frontera at the same time and place as Alonso Lobato and Cristobal Lobato. They are both recorded on a document that identified the expert seamen (Palermos) of Palos de La Frontera or neighbors of this area who departed to the new world during the period of exploration. [16] Cristobal Lobato was the Maestre of the Carabela, *La Concepcion* and a neighbor of Palos De La Frontera. A Maestre is the owner of a ship that comes from a prominent family with influence and money. Not only was he a wealthy and an educated merchant, but also an expert seaman. Cristobal Lobato was recorded as being the pilot of his ship. [17] He traveled with Pedro Arias Dávila who was in charge of the first expedition of discovery to the new world that departed in 1514 and arriving in Cuba in 1519. Cristobal Lobato then joined the Panfilio de Navarez expedition to Mexico from Cuba then joined the Hernan Cortes Expedition to conquer Mexico in 1520. [18]

In 1512, **Alonso Lobato** arrived in the West Indies with Diego Columbus, son of Christopher Columbus. The expedition of Diego Columbus was the only expedition from Palos de La Frontera that was recorded at this time. Diego Columbus set out for Hispaniola (Santo Domingo) after he was made the Governor of the West Indies, and after he was granted his father's rights and inherited his father's properties. Diego Columbus traveled with a huge envoy of family and friends including Pedro de Alvarado who arrived in Hispaniola in 1512. [19] Alonso Lobato was raised with Diego Columbus in Huelva, the place Christopher Columbus left him when he went on his expeditions of discovery.

Alonso Lobato

Diego Columbus was recalled to Spain by the King in 1514 after their relationship deteriorated. Alonso Lobato remained in Hispaniola (Santo Domingo) until he joined the expedition of Pedro Arias Dávila who arrived in the West Indies in 1514. Davila removed the acting Governor of the Indies and assumed his position as Governor of the Indies in Darien (Panama). [20]

Alonso Lobato was with Davila when he founded Panama City in 1519. Davila had a notary record the names of the soldiers present when he founded Panama City. Alonso Lobato was on this list which describes him as a man from Palos, an official man of the sea, and who arrived seven years ago. [21]

Three years after Panama City was founded, Davila applied the *Encomienda System* that was set up by the Spanish Crown. This system divided the American Indian labor force into groups that are to be used in the development of the mining economy. Under this system, a Spanish Conquistador, or another prominent male Spaniard (known as an Encomendero), is granted the labor of a certain number of Native Americans living in the area. The Encomendero provides protection to the laborers from warring tribes and provides them teachings in the Catholic faith. The native laborer paid tributes to the Encomendero in the form of gold or other metals, or agricultural products. [22] Alonso Lobato was identified on a list of Encomenderos in Panama dated 1522 as follows: *Alonso Lobato, a man of the sea and who has served 10 years in these parts, is awarded an Encomienda of eighty Chochama Indians that were entrusted to him.* [23]

In 1527, Alonso Lobato joined the failed expedition of Francisco Pizarro and Diego de Almagro from Panama to explore the boarder of South America.

(Portrait of Francisco Pizarro by Amable-Paul Coutan, 1835)

The sufferings on this expedition were more than the men could endure, so Pizarro sent Almagro back to Panama for food, ammunition, and reinforcements. Pizarro thought that Almagro would not return due to their last conflict, so he decided to send Carvallo with the pilot Bartolomé Ruiz to Panama on the other vessel that was disintegrating in the waters. With them, he sent Alonso Lobato, who was causing riots. At the time that they were embarking, Pizarro had to dissuade many, so that they did not seize the ship. If they had not been ill, Pizarro would have burned the boat, as Cortez did, so that no one would try to return or send messages. Seeing the second caravel vanish on the horizon, Pizarro was hopeless on the miserable island. His men were hungry and dying. A secret message in a poem was sent in a gift to the Governor's wife that she turned over to the Governor. The Governor brought Alonso Lobato, who came with Carvallo and the others who came with Almagro before him in order to question them. Alonso Lobato stepped forward and said: "*All the men who have stayed on Isla del Gallo want to return and would do so if Pizarro let them return.*" A vessel was then dispatched to bring back Pizarro and his men. Even though Almagro called these men cowards, Pizarro did not fault them because he had also suffered with them on the island. [24]

In 1529, Francisco Pizarro traveled to Spain and obtained permission from the Spanish Monarchy to conquer the land they called Peru after he encountered Indians in this area that possessed gold. Pizarro arrived in Peru in 1532 with an envoy of ships that he brought from Panama. This was the land of the Inca civilization. Pizarro captured their Emperor, Atahualpa, and demanded gold for his return. Even though his people paid the ransom, Pizarro and his men still executed Atahualpa which effectively ended the Inca Empire. [25]

(Picture courtesy of File:Machu Picchu, Peru.jpg - Wikimedia Commonsu)

In 1534, Alonso Lobato was awarded an Encomienda in Quito in Tatara (Yubos) which included 1000 tribe members and a pension of 1,000 pesos. This concession was made by Rodrigo de Salazar and Francisco Pizarro. [26] Francisco Pizarro and Almagro later engaged in a battle against each other over credit and recognition of the conquest of Peru. This was known as the Battle of Salinas where Pizarro captured and executed Almagro. Later, Almagro's son, Diego assassinated Pizarro in Lima, Peru. [27] Alonso Lobato remained in Quito and his son Don Francisco Lobato joined the silver miners in Potosi (upper Peru).

Don Francisco Lobato

Don Francisco Lobato invested in mining after the discovery of Cerro Rico de Potosi, (Alto Peru). Cerro Rico de Potosí was accidentally discovered in 1545 by Diego de Huallpa, a Quechua, while he was searching the Andean mountain for an Inca shrine or traditional burial offering. It is estimated that eighty-five percent of the silver produced in the central Andes during this time came from Cerro Rico. As a result of mining operations in the mountain, the city of Potosí became one of the largest cities in the New World [28]

(Description of Cerro Rico and the Imperial Municipality of Potosi - Gaspar Miguel de Berrio - WikiGallery.org, the largest gallery in the world)

In 1555, Francisco Lobato signed a contract of exploitation with Ortiz de Zarate in Potosi. They named the vein *"Veta de Don Francisco de Lobato."* [29] In 1585, Don Francisco Lobato still owned several mines in Cerro Rico de Potosi which are recorded as being owned by him, his heirs and his minors. [30]

(Picture courtesy of Epic World History: Potosí (Silver Mines of Colonial Peru))

Juan Lobato

In 1564, the deposits of Huancavelica in Peru were reported by the Indian Nahuincopa to his master Jerónimo Luis de Cabrera. The area was the most prolific source of mercury in Spanish America which was vital to the mining operations of the Spanish colonial era. Mercury was necessary to extract silver from the ores produced in the silver mines of Peru, as well as those of Potosí. [31] In 1567, Juan Lobato was registered as owning the rights of the east side of Huancavelica. [32] The family

of the original Encomenderos began to lose their rights granted to them for their services because they stopped living in the place corresponding to their assignment. This situation, in addition to the abuses against the natives, led the Crown to give these jurisdictions to those entrusted to inhabit the area as well as those who gave good treatment to the Indians. Also, The Holy Office of the Inquisition was installed in Peru in 1570 with the aim of preventing the deviations of the faith. They fought the Jews who converted to the Catholic faith that kept their old beliefs secret. They wanted to avoid their influence among the indigenous population. The Spanish Inquisition became an institution under the tutelage of the Spanish Crown. The power in Peru began to change and those in power began to lose their authority. [33]

The number of European-born Spaniards in the New World or Spaniards of pure blood who had been born in New Spain totaled no more than 250,000 people in 1600. This decline was due to the shift of resources to the Old World as they went to war with Europe. In the Spanish colonies, plantations, ranches, and mines became totally dependent upon slave labor imported from West Africa. With Spain no longer able to maintain its military control effectively over the Caribbean, the other Western European states finally began to move in and set up permanent settlements of their own, ending the Spanish monopoly over the control of the New World. [34]

Also, the huge Spanish silver shipments from the New World to the Old attracted pirates and French privateers both in the Caribbean and across the Atlantic. The Spanish could not afford a sufficient military presence to control such a vast area of ocean or enforce their exclusionary, mercantilist trading laws. These laws allowed only Spanish merchants to trade with the colonists of the Spanish Empire in the Americas. As colonies in the New World were badly neglected, Pirates pillaged and plundered the almost defenseless Spanish settlements with ease and with little interference from the European governments who had their own problems back home. The non-Spanish colonies were growing and expanding across the Caribbean. Many new immigrants settled into the West Indies' expanding plantation economy, while others took to the life of a buccaneer. [35]

Don Juan Lobato

In 1608, Juan Lobato was appointed as Alcalde Mayor of Mines in the Province of Honduras. Before his appointment took place, there was great alarm in the city because the current acting governor of the province sent an express request of militiamen to stop the pirates that again invaded Puerto Caballos which was north of Honduras. In 1609, Juan Lobato was appointed as the Alcalde Mayor of Honduras. [36] In 1617, Juan Lobato became the Governor of Honduras until 1620. [37] In 1621, Juan Lobato was sentenced by the Inquisition. [38]

The mining industry suffered greatly due to not having enough capital and labor, and by difficult terrain. Mercury, vital for the production of silver, was scarce and the mining industry no longer had representatives in the province. [39]

In 1617, A baptism record for Alonso Lobato was located that identifies Juan Lobato as his father and Mariana De Espinosa as his mother. The baptism took place in Santo Domingo, Sucre, Chuquisaca, Bolivia (Alto Peru). [40]

During this time, the war of the Basques and the Vicunas (non-Basque Spaniards) broke out in Alto Peru. This armed conflict lasted until 1625 which was a competition over the control of the silver mines in Potosi, Lipez and Chicas. The Vicuñas had initially employed legal and political measures attempting to block the Basque attempts to monopolize control over the Cabildo (municipal government) of Potosí and the silver mining sector. However, these efforts did not yield results. The conflict ended in mutual exhaustion with no victory. On March 15, 1626, the indigenous of Potosí were destroyed by a massive flood. [41] With the change in the municipal government, loss of Encomiendas, and the loss of most of the Indian population due to diseases and the great flood of Potosi, many miners moved on to mine other areas in Peru where silver was discovered.

Alonso Lobato

Silver was discovered in the Caylloma (south of Potosi in Peru) but even at its best, it never approached the importance of the great mines of Potosi and Hauncavelica. The production at Caylloma rose and fell and the rich mines were quickly depleted. Miners were forced to turn their attention elsewhere in Peru. In 1647, Alonso Lobato, who owned and worked the mill at Chipacha for sixteen years, reported that he was exploiting the rich mine of Tintamarca. He was also working the mine of Misagunca y Chinchon. He petitioned to leave Caylloma to establish a new mill in Tintamarca. Alonso Lobato was authorized to use sixty-two Caylloma Mitayos (*native indigenous*). [42]

Workers in the silver refining mills suffered the greatest exposure to mercury both in liquid and vapor forms which resulted in the widespread poisoning and death of countless people, including workers and other residents of Huancavelica, Potosí, and other mining centers. It was reported that there were frequent birth deformities, stillbirths, and mental illness. The mercury intoxication was causing aggressive and violent behavior that was expressed along ethnic and class lines. [43]

The next generation of the Lobato family chose to move on from mining in Peru and Bolivia to mining silver and exploring new lands in Mexico. Blas Lobato began this journey in 1662.

Blas Lobato

The Spanish Crown kept records of events that occurred in the West Indies in an archive named "*Pares Portal De Archivos Espanoles*," that recorded an event involving Blas Lobato in 1662 in Cartagena, Columbia. "Blas Lobato and Roque Gil, owners of the frigate (ship) '*Nuestra Señora de Regla y las Animas*,' assisted the *Audiencia de Santa Fé* in the seizure of an English yacht and its cargo when it entered the port of Cartagena in the frigate of the '*Nuestra Señora del Pópulo y las Animas*.'" (45)

As recorded, Blas Lobato moved on from Peru to the port of Cartagena on a ship that he owned which joined the fleet to Mexico. He then settled in Sombrerete, Mexico. A major silver strike occurred in Sombrerete, Mexico in 1646 that lasted until the end of the century. Sombrerete is located in a high valley in the northwestern state of Zacatecas.

Sombrerete established its own treasury office, and they kept records of events that contributed to its treasury. These records are stored in the *Archive of the State of Zacatecas*. A record for Blas Lobato was recorded in 1679 that places him in Sombrerete, Zacatecas, Mexico.

"In 1679, Blas Lobato from Sombrerete, Zacatecas Mexico who is the owner of the train near Sombrerete, was imprisoned in the city jail of Zacatecas, because he was sued by the owners of the land that his train traveled on. Blas Lobato and his partner, Juan de Leon, were accused of owing the following men: 350 pesos owed to Don Lucas Fernández Pardo, 300 pesos to Melchor Martínez, 300 pesos to Mr. Gerónimo de Villarreal, 104 pesos to Lucas Romero, and 35 pesos to Francisco de Salas. Blas Lobato agreed to pay all of them except for Lucas Fernández Pardo and Melchor Martinez, because he didn't owe them. He also agreed to pay the city of Zacatecas for imprisoning him in the city jail which included 170 pesos to the treasurer Francisco Gómez Rendón and 174 to the sheriff José de Villarreal. He was given two years to pay his debt and had to put up 35 mules for collateral." [46]

Also, an article was located that was published in the "Herencia" which was written by Rick Hendricks, Ph.D. which describes his brief visit to *Archivo Historico de Estado de Zacatecas* in 1992. He documents the discovery of pages that reveal information about the Blas Lobato family. One set of documents was executed in Sombrerete by Blas Lobato on August 18, 1679.

"The financial matters of Blas Lobato indicate that he may have been a man of some means. He put up his mulata slave, Felipa to secure a loan that he repaid. He was able to repay the loan because Felipa was no longer secured and sold six years later." The other set of documents reveal information about Blas Lobato, a New Mexico Settler who was the son of Blas Lobato. He was related to Bartolome Lobato and Matias Lobato who were also New Mexico settlers. [47]

Meanwhile, colonizers were sent to New Mexico to set up settlements. New Mexico is located in northern New Spain at the foot of the Sangre de Cristo Mountains, the southernmost subrange of the Rocky Mountains.

Don Juan de Onate was the first colonizer of New Mexico in 1598 with about 130 Spanish soldiers and their families. Later, another 80 soldiers and their families arrived which opened the way for priests and fryers, merchants, and colonists who entered New Mexico along El Camino Real from Mexico City and Chihuahua. In 1680, most of the Spaniards were driven out of New Mexico by the northern Pueblo Indians in the uprising known as the "Pueblo Revolt."

There were about 2,500 Spaniards in New Mexico before the majority of them fled south to El Paso. Some of the Spanish colonists remained in New Mexico in areas such as Santo Domingo, San Ildefonso and San Juan.

Those who stayed in New Mexico lived peacefully with the Pueblo Indians as long as they did not exert Spanish rule on them. In 1696, the new appointed Governor of New Mexico, Don Diego de Vargas, recolonized New Mexico with the exiled families and others recruited from Zacatecas, Mexico. [48]

Bartolome Lobato

A ledger of money paid out to families who agreed to volunteer to recolonize New Mexico was maintained by *His Majesty's Notary* and signed by Juan Paez Hurtado who recruited these families from Zacatecas, Mexico for Governor Vargas.

"List of families that accompanied Juan Paez Hurtado in 1695 on the fifth wave to Santa Fe: In the city of Nuestra Senora de los Zacatecos on 29 December 1694, Capt. Juan Paez Hurtado, for the purpose included in his Excellency's directives, brought the royal accounting house Bartolome Lobato, espanol, a native of the real mines of Sombrerete, twenty-nine, healthy, long, black hair, married to Luisana Negrete, espanola; and a one-year-old child named Juan, their son. They received 300 pesos in reals from the hands of the lord judges and treasury official in the captain's presence, who which I attest. The officials signed it with the captain." (49)

In 1696, Vargas issued a decree that ordered 19 of the 44 families that came from Zacatecas, to settle in the Villa of Santa Cruz. He gave them the same privileges and land grants that were awarded to the original settlers from Mexico City. Bartolome Lobato was not awarded land and remained in Santa Fe with the other families.

Bartolome Lobato had the means to purchase land from the settlers who did not want to remain in Santa Cruz due to hardships as indicated in a statement made by one of the settlers: *"My husband, Miguel de Zarate, myself, and my daughter, having been assigned to settle in this kingdom, it was determined to send us to the Villa Nueva de Santa Cruz to reside there, where, in the name of His Majesty, each one of the families was assigned a piece of land with which we could support ourselves by planting crops. For a long time, I remained settled in the said tract of land that was given to me in the name of the king, and finding my hardships increased, alone, a widow and without protection, I decided to move to this Villa de Santa Fe." Hernández sold her land to Bartolomé Lobato, a soldier who had served for ten years at the presidio in Santa Fe."* (50)

Many settlers from Zacatecas did not remain in Santa Cruz and returned back to Santa Fe due to the elements and the dangers arising from the rebellious Indians. In 1696, a rebellion occurred that attacked settlers from all directions. Despite weakness, Governor Vargas moved swiftly against the Indians. Roque Madrid was ordered to call in all missionaries while squads of men were sent on very dangerous missions to escort the friars back to the settlement. The uprising had taken the lives of 21 settlers and five missionaries. Churches and religious articles were burned.

"Since Juan de Archuleta was in the area, he decided to go to the Pueblo of San Juan de los Caballeros. He made the reverend Father, Fray Blas Navarro, who was closed up in his convento sleeping, and a soldier named Matias Lobato come out immediately. They collected the sacred vessels and vestments. The people had already abandoned the Pueblo and gone away. He left, bringing the reverend father, Fray Blas Navarro, and the soldier with him to Villa Nueva. He had left a saddled horse at the door." [49]

In 1697, a struggle over governorship of Santa Fe occurred between Vargas, the acting Governor and the viceroy appointed Governor, Pedro Rodriguez Cubero. In order to remove Vargas, Cubero accused him of embezzlement by making him liable for those he retained. In particular, Juan Paez who recruited volunteers in Zacatecas. Juan Paez was accused of committing fraud and embezzlement by his soldiers when they recruited for him.

"Bartolome Lobato, who had been appointed as a leader, stated that Juan Paez ordered him to seek out Spaniards who were vagrants and young men. In his capacity as leader, Lobato would accept the money at the treasury office and deliver it to Paez, who then paid them, 7 or 6 pesos and sent them away. Thirty people to whom this happened stated the same thing. Jose de Contreras, as secretary of government and war and servant of the company don Diego recruited, also corroborated this. Very few families received even 80 pesos. In his testimony, Lobato further added the circumstance that the families were forced to take goods at high prices in the shop belonging to Moya." [51]

Bartolome Lobato and his family were one of the few families that remained in the Santa Cruz settlement even when conditions drove many to return to Santa Fe. He continued to make peace with the natives as well as protect the settlers in Santa Cruz.

"Bartolome Lobato, Opinion, Cochiti Pueblo, 25 February, 1702, DS. I Sgt Bartolome Lobato, state that I have seen the proceedings prepared by don Pedro Rodriguez Cubero, lord governor and captain general of this kingdom and provinces of New Mexico and sustains in its presence for his majesty, in which he orders me to give my opinion about the is expressed therein. The twenty men included in the proceeding are very few. Thus, I am of the opinion that the lord

governor and captain general should send 34 more men for the safety of the priest who is in the pueblo. He can also order the cane returned to the Indian cacique, Don Juan, who is the one with the largest following and the person the Indians of Juni respect. Likewise, the alcalde mayor, Jose Narnajo, got along well with the cacique, Don Juan. According to the information that is circulating, the reason they are upset is that the cane was taken from him. In everything, the lord governor will decide what he sees fit. I signed it. Bartolome Lobato." [51]

In 1705, Governor Don Francisco Cuervo Y Valdes ordered a muster of the Santa Fe Presidio soldiers and local militias as soon as he took office. Eighty-three men from Santa Cruz presented themselves which included Bartolome Lobato. He noted that the families of Santa Cruz could not survive if further aid was not sent to them. A military campaign against the Apache and Navajo were sent out that resulted in a peace agreement that lasted several years. Santa Cruz was nearly abandoned when families moved on to more fertile areas near Chimayo. In order to bring the families to a more centralized area for protection, Cuervo y Valdes sanctioned the Villa de Santa Maria de Grado that was near their properties. This sanction was not approved by the royal officials because the central government and church were located in Santa Cruz. Twenty-nine residents of the Villa de Santa Maria de Grado signed a petition to have the church and office moved from Santa Cruz. One of the residents was Bartolome Lobato. [50]

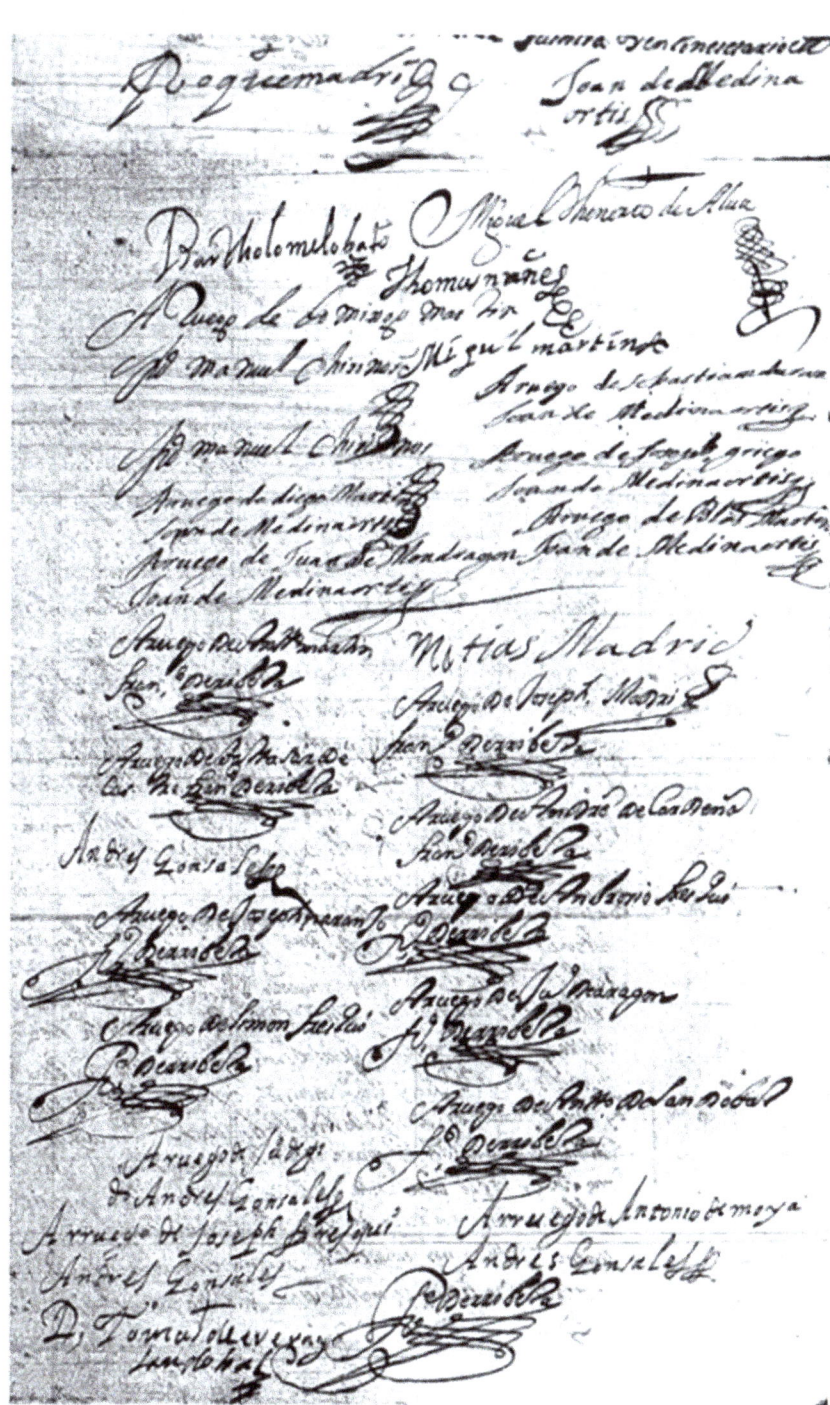

Signatures of the residents of the Villa de Santa María de Grado, vicinity of Chimayó, December 22, 1706. SANM II, no. 128.

The petition was rejected and the Villa de Santa Maria de Grado was not sanctioned. The area eventually became known as Chimayo. Santa Cruz eventually grew with the help of the church and central government. A census of Santa Cruz taken in 1707, lists Bartolome Lobato md. with Gertudis having 12 persons. He purchased land from Ramon Garcia Jurado in Santa Cruz in 1707.

In 1710, five residents of Santa Cruz petitioned for a grant of land that included the ruins of the very early Spanish settlement of San Gabriel del Yunque situated at the juncture of the Rio del Norte and the Chama River. In their petition, Captain Bartolomé Lobato, Captain Matías Madrid, Captain José Madrid, Captain Sebastián Durán, and Simón de Córdova asked for land to support themselves. The petition was granted then revoked. Two years later, the Captain General, Roque de Madrid, Blas Lobato and 4 others were added to the petition and resubmitted to the governor. [50]

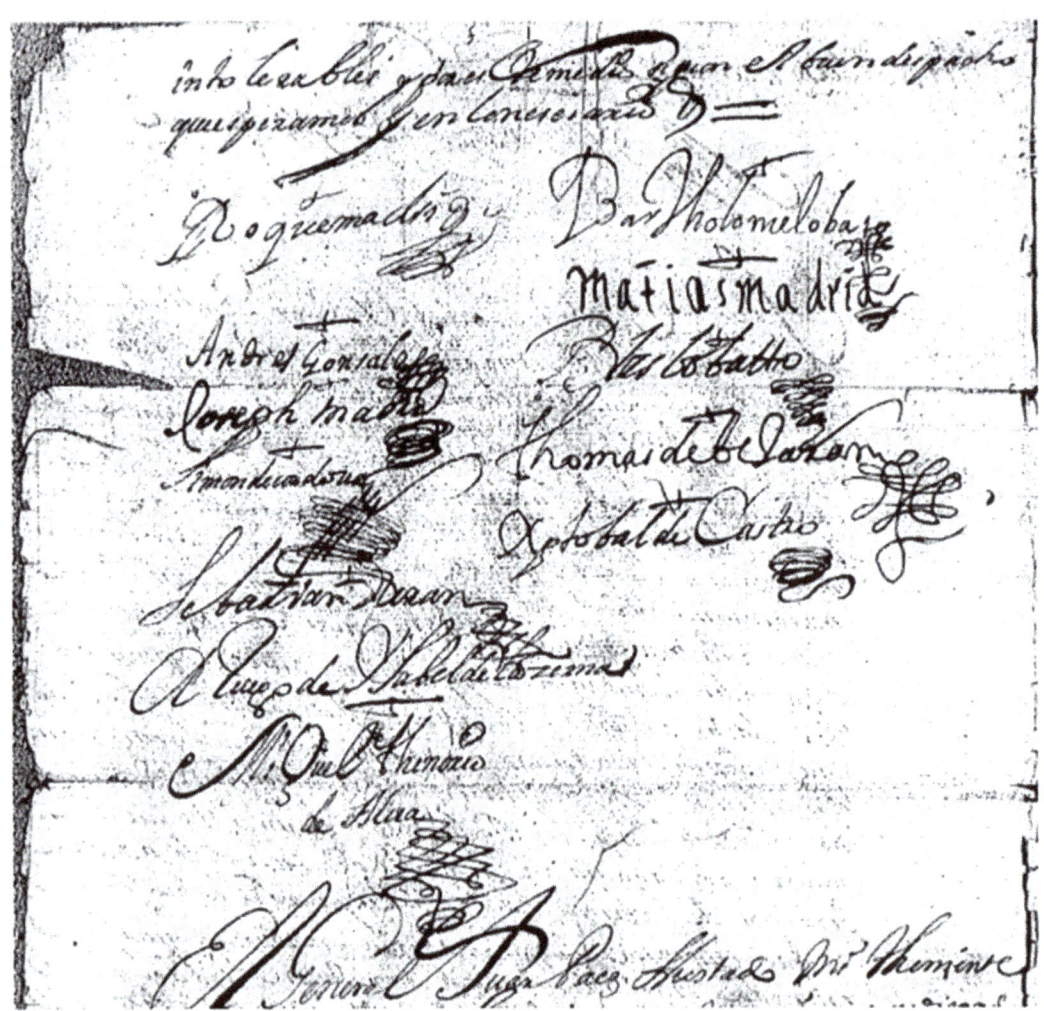

Signatures of individuals request land at the Puesto de Chama, 1712. SANM I, no. 1020, Juan de Ulibarrí, Bartolomé Lobato, Matías Madrid and Others, Petition for Lands near Puesto de Chama, 1710.

The petition was rejected on the grounds that all of the original settlers of Santa Cruz had sworn not to abandon the settlement of Santa Cruz which could not afford the depopulation of 11 families.

"Bartolomé Lobato, writing on behalf of the other petitioners, responded immediately to the denied request with particular attention to the statement made by Páez Hurtado that they had "sworn to settle the Villa Nueva de Santa Cruz since 1695." Responding directly to Lt. General Páez Hurtado, Lobato wrote: As it is known, to your Excellency that I entered among the number of the families from Zacatecas, and Cristóbal Rodarte [de Castro] and also Blas Lobato, my brother, came a long time after, and the Villa Nueva [de Santa Cruz] had already been founded and sworn to, and José Madrid and Matías Madrid, at the time of the [founding of the] said settlement, were soldiers of the company under your charge at the garrison of El Paso. Likewise, at the garrison at that time, serving their parents, were Diego Márquez and Simón de Córdova, whom your Excellency must have known, and Andrés González a soldier of this royal garrison, and Tomás Bejarano, a resident of this Villa de Santa Fe, and Sebastián Durán, also a resident of this Villa de Santa Fe." [51]

They were denied the petition once again even though their names could not be found on the documents created when Santa Cruz was established with the original settlers. Most of the settlers were living in poverty, but Bartolome Lobato had funds to pay laborers, purchase properties with houses, and purchase tools and livestock. According to Land Grant studies, the requested land grant of 1710 was later approved in 1714 after a new Governor took office. Bartolome Lobato purchased land from several parties as well as being awarded his own land grant.

"Bartolome Lobato owned a house in Santa Cruz and another in Santa Fe, as well as farming and grazing land in the Santa Cruz area and along the Chama River." [49]

> *"**424** JOSE CASTELLANOS to Bartolome Lobato. Santa Fe, August 8, 1701. Conveyance of house and land. Before Joseph Rodriguez, Alcalde. Testimonio certified to by the Alcalde. This also mentions the Rio Chiquito.*
>
> *425 JUANA DOMINGUEZ to Bartolome Lobato. Santa Fe, August 14, 1701. Conveyance of house and garden. Before Joseph Rodriguez, Alcalde. Lorenzo de Madrid, Joseph de Quintana. Says there is no notary within 270 leagues; refers also to the Rio Chiquito.*
>
> *427 RAMON GARCIA JURADO to Bartolome Lobato. Santa Cruz, May 7, 1707. Conveyance of land. Before Alphonso Rael de Aguilar, Alcalde. Xpttobal de Gongora, Antonio Duran de Armijo. A deed for a piece of land at Santa Cruz de La Canada, the boundaries being "on the north side by the river of said town (Villa) on that of the south by the said town.' 'This shows that when the Villa Nueva de Santa Cruz was reestablished by De Vargas in 1695, the same was on the south side; the present town of Santa Cruz is located on the north side of the river.*
>
> *433 BARTOLOME LOBATO. Grant. Situate on the Rio de Chama. 1714. Granted by Don Juan Ignacio Flores Mogollon, Governor and Captain-General. Possession given by Sebastian Martin, Alcalde. Re-validated in 1715 by Phelix Martinez, Governor; Miguel Thenorio de Alva, Secretary of Government and War. Roque de Pinto, Secretary of Government and War. Francisco de Carmona, Miguel de Quintana."* [52] *"Land allocated on the west side of Chama to Bartolome Lobato consists of a lot of land that includes two fanegas with a house, lot and garden which in their outskirts."* [53]

Bartolome Lobato was accompanied by his brother Matias Lobato, and later joined by his brother, Blas Lobato from Zacatecas. Matias is known for protecting a priest in a San Juan church during the Pueblo Revolt while other soldiers abandoned their posts and deserted. [54] Bartolome's son Juan Cayetano Lobato and his nephew, Blas Lobato also put their lives on the line to rescue and protect the Indians who became homeless and hungry.

"In 1716, Blas Lobato, a landowner and soldier who lived in the Atrisco area, joined the New Mexico troops that allied with Governor Felix Martinez on an expedition to rescue Indians who had fled from the Hopi lands. The homeless and hungry Indians were being brought back to resettle in the Christian Spanish Pueblo communities along the Rio Grande. Blas Lobato and Cayetano Lobato joined the Albuquerque contingency with five horses each and fully armed." [55]

Records for the early settlers in New Mexico from Zacatecas were lost, so accounting ledgers and other government documents have been used to distinguish who has descended from what family. For example, a younger Bartolome Lobato was documented as being either Bartolome's or Matias son because he was with them in Santa Cruz in 1705. There is no record of his birth parents, but a census taken in 1750 in Albuquerque classifies him as being Mulato, (Spanish and Black). Lucia Ana Negrete and the older Bartolome Lobato are both classified as being Spanish, so he was the son of Matias Lobato. The younger Bartolome was never awarded any land grants and moved to the Rio Abajo community.

"There were two men named Bartolome Lobato living in New Mexico at the same time. The older Bartolome Lobato was married to Lucia Ana Negrete, a native of Zacatecas. A much younger man was the husband of Juana Carrillo. Both Bartolomes and a Matias Lobato resided in Santa Cruz in 1705." [56] Years later, the younger Bartolome moved to Rio Abajo (Albuquerque) with a military transfer where two of his children are recorded in 1733 and 1734. He died at the age of 70 and was buried in the military chapel in Santa Fe on September 30, 1779. [57]

*"Bartholome Lobato, Mu, 60; wife, Juana Carrillo, Mu, 50, 2 daughters: Bisenta, 17, Rita, 15; 2 orphans: Barbara, Mu, Anna Maria, Mu, 6. Juan Thomas Lobato, Mu, Theadeo Lobato, Mu. *Mu=Mulato"* [58]

Juan Jose Lobato

When Captain Juan Paez Hurtado took accounting of those who went to New Mexico with him from Zacatecas, he described Bartolome Lobato as being 29 on December 29, 1694, married to Luisana Negrete, and having a one-year-old child named Juan, their son. Based on this information, Juan Lobato was born in 1693 in Zacatecas, Mexico. His brother, Juan Cayetano Lobato was born in 1698 and his brother Augustin Lobato was born in 1703. [49]

The book *Origins of New Mexico Families: A Genealogy of the Spanish Colonial Period*, identifies another Lobato child as belonging to either Bartolome Lobato or Matias Lobato. "*Other children of Bartolome or Matias Lobato are Juan (Jose) Lobato, married to Elena Martin at San Juan, Rio Arriba, New Mexico on November 27, 1733. Their son Agustin was born at Ojo Caliente September 5, 1746.*" [59]

Juan Jose Lobato remained in the Chama, Rio Arriba area with Bartolome Lobato and set out to add more land to their current land grant holdings. "*By the 1720s, the Spanish government initiated formal land grants on previously unsettled lands up the Valle del Rio Chama. These small kin-based Placitas of former soldiers and their families were the farthest frontier outposts of the Viceroyalty of Spain, which could afford them little military protection. Defense against nomadic attack was among these settlers first concern, and it was natural for a prominent military man to become a settlement's leader.*" [60]

Juan Jose Lobato began his career as a servant to King of Spain by becoming a Notary in Santa Fe in 1723. He was recorded as being a witness as a notary on several marriage records found in the *Archives of the Archdiocese of Santa Fe*.

In 1733, a tract of land on the Chama River was placed in the royal possession of Captain Cristobal Torres, but it was forfeited because he didn't take possession of it before he died as required by *Royal Law*. After the grant was revoked, the land was placed in the possession of Juan Jose Lobato and Diego de Torres, son of Cristobal Torres. That grant was later revoked because Juan Jose Lobato sold his interest in the land which was forbidden by *Royal Laws*. Juan Jose Lobato petitioned for a new grant covering the same area and promised to comply with the *Royal Law* of settling on it. Once again, the grant was awarded to Juan Jose Lobato in 1740. In 1744, the Governor asked Juan Jose Lobato to vacate the land because his grant included the land belonging to Mestas. Cristobal Torres had previously cleared the title of this land without the objection of Mestas before he died, so Juan Jose objected to the eviction and provided this proof. The grant was validated based on the clear title. Juan Jose Lobato and his heirs took possession of the land and occupied it as required by *Royal Law*. The land grant contained 205,215.72 acres. [61]

In 1750, a census of Spanish families living in La Neustra Senora de la Soledad del Rio del Norte Arriba was taken, and Juan Jose Lobato, his wife, Elena Martin, and his family were recorded as living in this protected community. This land was owned by Elena Martin's family. It was a ranch built like an outpost that was fortified with hefty construction to provide defense against the Apache and Comanche Indians. The house had thick walls of adobe, twenty-four rooms, and two protective towers. [62]

The Census is as follows: *"El Captain Don Juan Joseph Lovato (Lobato); Dona Elena Martines; Juan Domingo; Maria Barbara; Antonio Joseph; Cristobal Lorenzo de la Cruz; Michaela Franca; Juan Augustin de Jesus; Maria Rosa; servants: Petronila; Getrudis."* [63]

In 1750, Juan Jose Lobato was appointed Alcalde Mayor, a traditional Spanish municipal magistrate having both judicial and administrative functions of Santa Cruz. In 1751, he was an attorney, Chief Justice, and War Captain of the jurisdiction of Nuestra Senora de la Soledad del Rio Arriba. He was also the attending judge in the absence of public or royal notaries within the limits provided by law. *"Juan Jose Lobato, the alcalde mayor of Santa Cruz, was given the thankless task of convincing the Chama colonists that resettlement was a safe and viable choice. Alcalde Lobato had to resort to threats of house and land title forfeiture, as well as to attacks on the settlers' pride, before he could persuade even a handful to return to the abandoned plazas along the Chama River."* [64]

In 1751, Governor Tomas Veles Cachupín conveyed land to 12 families near Santa Fe, New Mexico due to the shortage of land and water in Santa Fe. It was a community grant known as *Las Trampas Grant*. Alcalde Juan Jose Lobato was instructed to divide and give possession of the land to the individual families. Even though the families settled on the land, they soon moved out due the dangers of Indian raids but continued to herd sheep on it seasonally. They returned for a short time in order to keep ownership of the land titles. [60]

In 1777, Juan Bautista de Anza was appointed Governor of New Mexico. He forced the scattered communities to consolidate into a fortified town for protection. Anza then organized a troop of 600 soldiers and 200 Utes and defeated the Comanches in Colorado. During that time, a severe drought reduced the wildlife and crops causing starvation among the remaining tribes. Anza offered help to these tribes by promising them food or relocating them to the Pueblos if they would join him.

By 1781, the Pueblo Indians had allied with the Spanish against the nomadic and raiding Apache, Comanches, Utes, and Navajos. They also supported the Spanish during the war with England, but only about 10,000 survived after the smallpox epidemic. The tribes also began to war against each other which drove some away to the mountains of Texas and California. Others began to raise sheep like the Spanish and trade with other tribes as well as the Spanish of New Mexico. Even though the Apache raided many Spanish settlements, they left the settlers of New Mexico alone because they were their customers who traded with other tribes, and because they had fortified towns with soldiers.

Even though Anza made peace with most of the tribes, he could not move forward with his plans to create a trade route between New Mexico and California. The Yumas who occupied that route, massacred the soldiers, settlers, and priests from a newly established settlement along the route. Anza also had to contribute supplies, money, and soldiers to Spain when they declared war against England. After the war with England ended in 1783, Anza established a trade route between Santa Fe, Texas, and Louisiana by making peace with the Comanche that occupied that route.

A list of names was kept of those who contributed to the war with England. The money donations exceeded a million pesos. Many soldiers also donated their militia salaries. Names of those who contributed were identified by their settlements or tribes. In New Mexico, the settlements were organized into 8 areas, Santa Fe, Santa Cruz de la Canada, Taos, Keres, San Carlos de Alameda, Albuquerque, Laguna and Zuni. Landowners tended to be heads of militia. Pueblo Indians had their own militia who were not identified individually by name. Genfzaros were Christian Indians that were raised in Spanish homes that spoke Spanish and lived in a separate community who also served as soldiers and militia. Indian tribe warriors also served who received property and supplies as their pay. Only names of their Chiefs are known.

"A list of those who contributed to the war voluntary fund: Cristobal Lorenzo Lobato (Spanish), 49 and Maria Armijo, 37, Taos. (1790 Census)" [64]

Cristobal Lorenzo de la Crus Lobato

(Cristobal Lorenzo Lobato, Cristobal Lobato, Lorenzo Lobato, Christoval Lobato)

Cristobal Lorenzo de la Cruz Lobato was the son of Juan Jose Lobato and Maria Elena Serrano and lived in the Chama, Rio Arriba area as indicated by the 1750 census. [63] Also, Angelico Chavez who documented genealogical data of matrimonial investigations found in the *Archives of the Archdiocese of Santa Fe*, recorded a wedding that references Cristobal Lobato from the Chama, Rio Arriba area (location of the Bartolome and Juan Jose Lobato land grants). This record documents the marriage of Juan Isidro Lobato, the son of Cristobal Lobato and Juana Mestas from San Jose de Chama. The age and date of Juan Isidro's marriage indicate that he was born in 1778. [65] Also, a record for Maria Luz Lobato was located with the following information: "*Christening Date: 15 Aug 1784, Christening Place: Santa Clara, Rio Arriba, New Mexico, Birthplace: Chama, Father's Name: Christoval Lobato, Mother's Name: Juana Mestas.*" [66]

In 1784, Cristobal Lorenzo Lobato was one of the witnesses on the will for Francisco Martin in San Antonio de Embudo. [67] San Antonio de Embudo was a fortified settlement that was a mile east of the Rio Grande in a well-watered valley. It provided a line of defense for the colony against the raiders. Like most of the Spanish villages, it was abandoned by 1748 due to the dangerous Indian attacks. Land Grant owners returned after they were told do so or they would forfeit their land claims. As settlements from the south expanded north, Embudo became a key trade center near the Picuris Pueblo, Taos Pueblo and Ranchos de Taos. [68]

By 1789, Cristobal Lorenzo Lobato relocated to the Taos area and remarried at the age of 48 to Maria Gregoria Armijo. [64] Several records were also located that document either Cristobal or Lorenzo Lobato with his wife Maria Armijo as sponsors or witnesses for baptisms or marriages that took place in the Taos Pueblo.

"9 Aug 1789 Juana Maria Dolores, born 27 Jul 1789 in the pueblo, daughter of Santiago Lujan and Maria Gavilan, Indians of the pueblo. Sponsors Lorenzo Lobato and his wife, Maria Armijo, residents of this pueblo. 10.1.1793 Maria Getrudes born 9.30.1793 daughter of Jose Sanches and Maria Antonia Antonia Xaramillo. Sponsors Lorenzo Lobato and Maria Gregoria Armijo." [69]

In 1796, Don Lorenzo Lobato and Don Antonio Joseph Lobato (sons of Juan Jose Lobato) accompanied the Alcalde Mayor and War Captain of Taos, Don Antonio Joseph Ortiz, who awarded 63 families possession of the fortified community, El Rio De Don Fernando (Taos). [70] Cristobal Lorenzo Lobato lived in Taos in 1797 as indicated by his arrest for trading with the Ute Indians.

*"**Punishment for Trade with Ute Indians-1797** These men included Cristóval Lovato, José Miguel Narajo, Juan Domingo Sandoval, José Martín, Andrés Martín, Juan Ballejos, Asensio Lucero, Juan Esteban Velásquez, Gabriel Vígil, Nerio Gómez, Francisco Salazar, Mateo García, Nicolás Martín, Pedro Sisneros, Ramón Saiz, Antonio Maese, Francisco Archuleta, José Manuel Montoya, Silvestre López, Juan de Dios Trujillo, Antonio Torres, Pedro Aguilar, Antonio José Espinosa and Juan Griego. When one of the lead traders, Cristóbal Lobato of Taos was asked if he realized that expeditions to the Yuta country were illegal, he answered, recognizing the illegality, but that his "debts made him trespass there." While they were all punished according to the violation, the punishment must have been minimal since subsequent records reveals that many of these same men continued to trade with the Yutas, as far north as the Great Basin. Many of these men became the vehicles for the exchanges of Indian captives, primarily making the exchange with the Yutas, then bringing them back to the community and other households, not necessarily holding them themselves, but presumably exchanging them for their own debts."* [71]

Juan Isidro Lobato

Juan Isidro Lobato was born in 1778 and married Maria Beatriz Salazar in 1798 in San Jose de Chama, New Mexico. Records of his children, Jose Antonio Hipolito "Polito" Lobato, Maria Concepcion Lobato and Antonio Nero Lobato were located in the *Pre-Nuptial Investigations (1678-1869) of the Archives of the Archdiocese of Santa Fe.* [65] A record for their son Juan Christoval Lobato was found in the collection of *New Mexico Marriages 1751-1918.* [72]

Juan Isidro and his family remained in the Santa Clara, Rio Arriba New Mexico area on the Bartolome and Juan Jose Lobato grant. When the heirs of the Juan Jose Lobato grant petitioned to have it reconfirmed, the sons of Juan Isidro Lobato, Juan Cristobal and Polito Lobato were verified as being the heirs of Juan Jose Lobato.

"Using land grant documents, baptism, marriage and death records, we were able to piece together and trace the family histories of eight of the eleven petitioners. Juan Cristobal and Polito Lobato comprised the final sibling set, whose great grandfather was Juan Jose Lobato the Alcalde Mayor who terminated the Herrera-Jaramillo grant in the 1760's." [72]

In 1823, Charles Beaubien, a Canadian arrived in Taos, New Mexico, and married Maria Paula Lobato. In 1841, he acquired a 1.7-million-acre land grant in Colorado which included the San Luis Valley. The town of San Luis is located on southeastern part of the San Luis Valley on the border of Colorado and New Mexico. It is a 122-mile-long and 74-mile-wide valley that sits in the south-central part of Colorado. It is enclosed by the San Juan and Sangre de Cristo Mountain ranges. The elevation is about 7800 feet above sea level making it the highest alpine desert valley in North America.

In 1847, as landlord of the Sangre de Cristo land grant, Beaubien began his first effort to create the first settlements on the land. He offered settlers a deed as compensation as well as use of common lands for grazing their livestock. The land at this time was still part of Mexico until 1848 when it became part of the Treaty of Guadalupe Hidalgo that was signed by Mexico and the United States. This treaty ended the U.S.-Mexican War. The treaty promised to uphold the land rights of Mexican settlers as well as making them citizens of the United States. The treaty also led to the construction of Ft. Massachusetts which was located 15 miles north of the town of San Luis to protect these citizens against the Apache and Ute Indians in the area.

In 1850, Beaubien began with small settlements along the Costilla River. These settlements are known as San Acacio, San Pablo, San Pedro, Chama, and San Francisco. There were about 1,800 people added to the grant as property holders including Juan Cristoval Lobato, son of Juan Isidro Lobato. [73]

Juan Cristoval Lobato

Juan Cristoval Lobato was born in 1804 and married Maria Del Rosario Alijabu in 1829 in Santa Clara, Rio Arriba, New Mexico. Records of their sons, Manuel Antonio Pantaleon Lovato and Jose Francisco Lobato were located in the collection of *New Mexico Births and Christenings, 1726-1918.*

"Name: Juan Christobal Lovato, Spouse: Alexabu, Event Date: 03 Oct 1829, Place: Santa Clara, Rio Arriba, New Mexico, Father: Juan Isidro Lovato, Mother: Beatris Salazar

Name: Manuel Antonio Pantaleon Lovato, Christening Date: 29 Jul 1743, Place: Santa Clara, Rio Arriba, New Mexico, Father: Juan Cristobal Lobato, Mother: Maria Del Rosario Alijabu

Name: Jose Francisco Lovato, Spouse: Maria Antonia De La Luz Ortega, Event Date: 05 Feb 1855, Place: San Juan Arriba, New Mexico, Father: Juan Cristoval Lobato, Mother: Maria Del Rosario Alijabu" [74]

An old tombstone of Cristoval Lobato (1804-1882) has been located on the hills of San Pablo, Colorado (about 2 miles east of the town of San Luis, Colorado). Photo below is of Cristoval Lobato with his great grandson, Moises Lobato, my father.

This branch of the "Lobato Family" has remained in San Luis, Colorado (and the surrounding small communities) since it was founded in 1850. Juan Cristoval Lobato was the first settler from this family. He lived for 80 years until 1882. He passed down land located 6 miles east of San Luis to his heirs that still remains in the family. This land is known as "Canyon" which has never been partitioned off to individual family members, so members of the family share its resources and have preserved it in its original form. The families gather on the land for camping, fishing, and holidays. They grow hay on it and bail it for the farm animals.

Jose Francisco Lobato

Jose Francisco Lobato, son of Juan Cristoval Lobato and Maria Del Rosario Alijabu was born in 1836 and married Maria Antonia De La Luz Ortega in 1855 in San Juan, Rio Arriba, NM. They had one child named Jose Francisco Lobato.

"Wedding of: Name: Jose Francisco Lovato, Spouse: Maria Antonia De La Luz Ortega, Event Date: 05 Feb 1855, Place: San Juan Arriba, New Mexico, Father: Juan Cristoval Lobato, Mother: Maria Del Rosario Alijabu" [74]

"Name: Jose Francisco Lovato Jr., Christening Date: 25 Jul 1861, Christening Place: San Juan, Rio Arriba, New Mexico, Birth Date: 22 Jul 1861, Birthplace: Ojo Caliente, Father's Name: Jose Francisco Lovato, Mother's Name: Maria Antonia De La Luz Ortega (New Mexico Births and Christenings, 1726-1918." [75]

Jose Francisco Lobato joined the military in 1831 when he was 25 years old. He joined on the side of the Union during the Civil War. [76]

Jose Francisco Lobato Jr.

Jose Francisco Lobato Jr. was born on July 22, 1861, in Ojo Caliente, Rio Arriba, New Mexico Territory, US. He married Maria De La Cruz Sanchez (Crusita) in 1879 in San Luis, Colorado. Jose Francisco Lobato and Crusita Sanchez had eight children: Emilio Lobato, Elvira Vialpando, Enrique Lobato, Adelaido Lobato, Andres Lobato, Edisia Lobato, Adrian Lobato, Felipe Vialpando and Presentacion Lobato. They established their home in Chama, Colorado. (4 miles southeast of San Luis, Colorado). [77]

State of Colorado
Division of Vital Statistics   No. Unknown

MARRIAGE RECORD REPORT

County........Costilla

Husband's Name...Lobato Jose Francisco....Age..Unknown.Race...White

Wife's Name.....Sanchez Maria De La C.,....Age..Unknown.Race.White

Place of Marriage........Chama, Colo.,.....................Date..10/21/1879

Name of Official who Performed Ceremony......Rev. Robert Garasu

Title ...Catholic Priest..Address.........San Luis, Colo.

Reported by.........Willie Lobato

Address ....San Luis, Colo.

50M—3-31-39—BRADFORD-ROBINSON, DENVER

In 1905, Jose Francisco also owned a mercantile store in Chama, Colorado.

Three of Jose Francisco Lobato's Children: Adrian, Elvira, and Jose Presentacion Lobato

Jose Presentacion Lobato

Jose Presentacion Lobato (Penta) was born April 12, 1905, and married Ernestina Sanchez in 1929. They lived in Chama, Colorado and they had twelve children: Jose, Carlos, Eva, Ernestine, Jenny, James, Presentacion (June), Bonifacio, Marcos, Adolph, Juan, and Moises Lobato. [78]

Jose Presentacion Lobato was drafted into the military in 1940.

A picture of six of the children of Jose Presentacion Lobato and Ernestina Sanchez around 1941 which include from left to right: Eva, Jennie (front), Carlos, Bonifacio, Moises, Jose Francisco, and their beloved dog Fido.

Jose Presentacion Lobato and his family lived on the Canyon Ranch for many years before moving to Chama, Colorado. Remains of the home that they lived in can still be found on the Canyon Ranch. (Pictured sons) Jose, Bonifacio, Marcos, Adolfo, and Moises Lobato

A picture of Jose Presentacion and Ernestine Lobato.

Ernestina Sanchez, wife of Jose Presentacion Lobato, was born in 1910 in El Rito de San Francisco, Colorado. Ernestina was the daughter of Elvira Taylor and Carlos Sanchez. Elvira Taylor comes from a Jewish family that emigrated from Germany to New Mexico. [79]

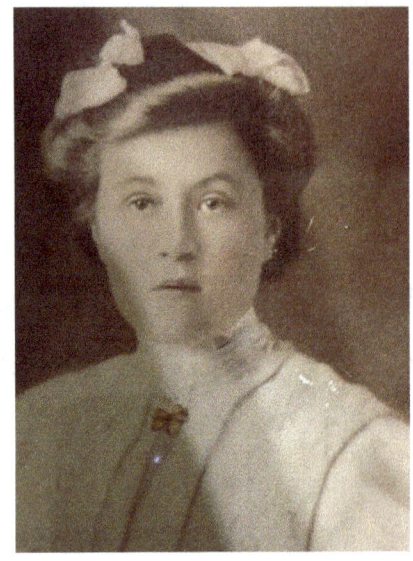

Moises Lobato

Moises Lobato, my father, was born on January 10, 1935, in Chama, Colorado and married Rita Vigil in the Sangre De Cristo Church in San Luis, Colorado on June 9, 1963. Moises and Rita Lobato currently live in San Luis, Colorado and own a portion of the original Sangre de Cristo Land Grant known as Canyon. All of the Moises Lobato family have access to the resources on the mountain range that is known as "Taylor's Ranch" that was also a part of the Sangre de Cristo Land Grant. All the heirs have a letter and key that gives them access to the mountain resources.

Moises and Rita Lobato have three children, Andrew Lobato, Christine Lobato-Ross and Charlotte Gomez.

Moises Lobato was born and raised on the Canyon Ranch and in Chama, Colorado until he was 15 years old when he moved to Fort Garland, Colorado with his aunt and uncle, Sam, and Emma Medina. His Uncle Sam taught him how to harvest hay and assisted him with the purchase his first farming equipment. He seasonally worked in the potato fields with his brothers.

Moises Lobato was drafted into the army in 1958. He was in the Army Reserves with over 100 men who were put through rigorous testing. They only selected 10 of the men to add to a special unit and he was one of them selected. Since the United States was at a time of peace, they sent him home until further notice, but he was never recalled.

Moises Lobato enjoyed boxing for sport. He recalls defeating a boxer in a local match who later won the Golden Glove Championship in Denver, Colorado. He later became a lumberjack in New Mexico. He also raised sheep and cattle and grew most of his crops. He hunts deer and elk for the meat and picks pinon nuts when in season.

Moises Lobato is currently the oldest living sibling in his family. He still hunts deer during hunting season. He's the grandfather of five and great grandfather of five.

Christine Dianne Lobato-Ross

I was born in La Jara, Colorado (31 miles West of San Luis, Colorado) to Moises & Rita Lobato who live in San Luis, Colorado.

I received a full academic scholarship to New Mexico Highlands University where I earned a bachelor's degree in accounting. I accepted a job with The Department of Defense Audit Agency at Lockheed Martin in Denver, Colorado. I met my husband, Demetrius Ross in Denver, Colorado. We were married in 1992 and have two sons, Demetrius Moses 7 Ross who was born in 1998 and Christian Angelo Ross who was born in 2001. Demetrius Ross Sr. is a Manager for Raytheon's Intelligence and Space Division. He has worked on rockets for NASA, Lockheed Martin, and Boeing. Demetrius Ross Jr. is attending the University of Colorado in Boulder and seeking a degree in Aerospace Engineering and Computer Science. Christian is working towards a Degree in Computer Programming while running his own Cybersecurity company, Alientec.

Christian Angelo Ross   Demetrius Moses 7 Ross

Conclusion

Discovering that my Lobato name is a Jewish name made me wonder where I came from. I always had assumed that my family historically was of the Christian faith. While researching my ancestry and discovering the Jewish ties, I found out that I may be able to gain citizenship if I could prove my family was expelled. The Jewish Federation of New Mexico was created to help a person prove their Sephardic Jewish heritage so that they can apply for citizenship in Spain. This process is a difficult process for many from Colorado and New Mexico because their surnames changed many times throughout history. Since the Lobato name has always been passed down and preserved throughout history, I was able to make a strong case about my heritage. After providing compelling evidence, the Jewish Federation of New Mexico issued me a certificate stating that I am of Sephardic Jewish heritage and descend from those families who were unjustly expelled from Spain or forced to convert to Christianity since 1492. Unfortunately, they informed me that I cannot apply for citizenship in Portugal because the Jewish Community of Oporto only accepts those who are currently of the Jewish faith, which I was not. The process for Spain had a time limit, so I submitted my application to the Jewish Community of Oporto in Portugal anyway and they rejected me because I was not a practicing orthodox Jew. I replied to their rejection by reminding them that my family name is Jewish and originated in Spain/Portugal. The Spanish Inquisition followed my family to America, so they had to convert to Catholicism to avoid religious persecution. At that time, the Inquisitors were burning Jews at the stake or imprisoning them for life. Also, Jews were not allowed to own land or businesses. After my family converted, their Jewish faith was forgotten over time. After making my case, I was approved. According to the Jewish Federation of New Mexico, I am the only non-Jewish applicant who has been approved from our region.

I always questioned why my birth certificate states that my race is white. This was also passed down because my family lived on the same land in Colorado that first belonged to Spain, then Mexico and finally to the United States.

I always wondered why my family was willing to endure hardships in new settlements and expose themselves to dangerous situations rather that live in established areas. I discovered that the Lobato name was always a target because it was on the Inquisition list, and it was not a common name. The Lobato name came through the route of South America to Mexico, New Mexico, and finally Colorado. When in New Mexico, my family was not awarded any land, so they bought it from other settlers. After gaining land and established positions, they were awarded land grants.

The Lobato name was not common in the New World but very common in Spain and Portugal. They aided the King of Spain in the reconquest and helped the King of Portugal in many of their wars. The history of my family before Spain needs to be explored further. These knights that come from the Holy Land are known to be part of the Knights Templars or similar organizations. I'm excited to see where further research with take me as well as tying my mother's family to the Basques and the Royal families of Spain. This book is only the beginning.

References

[1]Richard Gottheil, Kaufmann Kohler, Marcus Jastrow, Louis Ginzberg, Duncan B. McDonald. "BENJAMIN - JewishEncyclopedia.Com," The unedited full-text of the Jewish Encyclopedia 1906. http://www.jewishencyclopedia.com/articles/2947-benjamin.

[2]"The Name LOBATO | BH Open Databases." Museum of The Jewish People - Beit Hatfutsot. Accessed October 10, 2019. https://dbs.bh.org.il/familyname/lobato.

[3] Elmer Martinez. *LOBATO ORIGINALES EXPANOLES, Who Referenced Enciclopedia Ilustrada Universal, Madrid, Garcia Carraffa, Enciclopedia Heraldica, Madrid*. Spanish History Publications, n.d.

[4] ciudad-real.es. "La Heraldica de los Apellidos," 2003. http://www.ciudad-real.es/varios/heraldica/buscar.php?ape=Lobato.

[5]"Familia Lobato, heráldica, genealogía, escudo y origen appellido." Heraldrys Institute of Rome. Accessed September 23, 2019. https://www.heraldrysinstitute.com/lang/es/cognomi/Lobato/Espa%26ntilde%3Ba/idc/609987/

[6]Baêna, Miguel Sanches "de." *Indice heraldico: ou descripcao completa das armas de todas as familias que em Portugal tiveram e regstraram cartas de Brazao de armas organisado com referencia ao Archivo heraldico genealogico*. Antunes, 1872.

[7]"Pedro Eanes Lobato - Portugal, Dicionário Histórico." Accessed September 25, 2019. http://www.arqnet.pt/dicionario/eaneslo.html.

[8]References are found on website (*general background information*): "John I of Portugal." In *Wikipedia*, August 7, 2019. https://en.wikipedia.org/w/index.php?title=John_I_of_Portugal&oldid=909715859.

[9]AEPEL. "PEDRO EANES LOBATO." Accessed September 25, 2019. http://www.agrupamentopedroeaneslobato.pt/patrono.html.

[10]Varzeano, José. "Correio Das Lembranças: Pedro Eanes Lobato." *Correio Das Lembranças* (blog), July 12, 2012. http://memoriasdomeubairro.blogspot.com/2012/07/pedro-eanes-lobato.html.

[11] References are found on website (*general background information):* "Conquest of Ceuta." In *Wikipedia*, September 20, 2019. https://en.wikipedia.org/w/index.php?title=Conquest_of_Ceuta&oldid=916820587.

[12] References are found on website (*general background information):* "Prince Henry the Navigator." In *Wikipedia*, September 8, 2019. https://en.wikipedia.org/w/index.php?title=Prince_Henry_the_Navigator&oldid=914638499.

[13]"Portugal - CIRCA 1998 A Stamp Printed in Portugal Shows Captain.." 123RF. Accessed September 27, 2019. https://www.123rf.com/photo_25261577_portugal-circa-1998-a-stamp-printed-in-portugal-shows-captain-francisco-lobato-faria-and-sea-god-nep.html.

[14]Subrahmanyam, Sanjay. *The Career and Legend of Vasco Da Gama*. Cambridge University Press, 1998.

[15]Urueta, José P. *Documentos para la historia de Cartagena*. Tip. de Araújo, 1887.

[16]Labrado, Julio IZQUIERDO. "LA EMIGRACION PALERMA A AMERICA," no. Palos de la Frontera (2009): 17.

[17] García, María del Carmen Mena. *Sevilla y las Flotas de Indias: la Gran Armada de Castilla del Oro (1513-1514)*. Universidad de Sevilla, 1998.

[18] Gary Felix. "The Genealogy of Mexico GATEWAY TO THE PAST FROM OUR ANCESTORS FORWARD." Accessed September 29, 2019. http://garyfelix.tripod.com/~GaryFelix/index2.htm#Lobato.

[19] Polu Sifontes, Francis, and Francis Polu Sifontes. "Título de Alotenango, 1565: Clave p'allugar Xeográficamente l'antigua Itzcuintepec Pipil." *Antropoloxía y Hestoria de Guatemala* 3, Dómina II (n.d.).

[20] References are found on website *(general background information)*: "Pedro Arias Dávila." In *Wikipedia*, September 16, 2019. https://en.wikipedia.org/w/index.php?title=Pedro_Arias_D%C3%A1vila&oldid=916072135.

[21] Mario Gongoro. "LOS GUPOS DE CONQUISTADORES EN TIERRA FIRME (1509-1530), Fisonomia Historical-Social De Un Tipo De Conquista." *UNIVERSIDAD DE CHILE CENTRO DE HISTORIA COLONIAL*, 1962.

[22] "The Encomienda System: APUSH Topics to Study for Test Day." Magoosh High School Blog, October 10, 2017. https://magoosh.com/hs/apush/2017/encomienda-system-apush-topics/.

[23] Mª del Carmen Mena García. "1.- LA REFORMA DE LA ENCOMIENDA PANAMEÑA POR PEDRARIAS DÁVILA FUENTE PARA SU ESTUDIO." *TEMAS AMERICANISTAS*, 1990, 1–29.

[24] Carlos J. Sánchez; M.D., B.S., FAAP. "EL RAPTO DE NUESTRO CONTINENTE,EL HOLOCAUSTO DE TODOS LOS TIEMPOS, EL GENOCIDIO DE LOS INCAS EL ANIQUILAMIENTO DE LOS 'INDIOS.'" Accessed October 1, 2019. http://www.kuntursoul.org/LibroHolocaustoDeTodosLosTiempos-Espanol.pdf.

[25] References are found on website *(general background information)*: "Francisco Pizarro." In *Wikipedia*, September 24, 2019. https://en.wikipedia.org/w/index.php?title=Francisco_Pizarro&oldid=917499415.

[26] References are found on website *(general background information)*: "Spanish Conquest of Peru." In *Wikipedia*, October 2, 2019. https://en.wikipedia.org/w/index.php?title=Spanish_conquest_of_Peru&oldid=919174425.

[27] Ducasse, Javier Ortiz de la Tabla. *Los encomenderos de Quito, 1534-1660: origen y evolución de una elite colonial*. Editorial CSIC - CSIC Press, 1993.

[28] "Francisco Pizarro." Biography. Accessed September 22, 2019. https://www.biography.com/explorer/francisco-pizarro.

[29] Ana Marfa Presta M. A. "ENCOMIENDA, FAMILY, AND BUSINESS IN COLONIAL CHARGAS (MODERN BOLIVIA). THE ENCOMENDEROS OF LA PLATA, 1550-1600," 1997. https://etd.ohiolink.edu/!etd.send_file?accession=osu1487946776024292&disposition=inline.

[30] References are found on website *(general background information)*: "Cerro Rico." In *Wikipedia*, August 19, 2019. https://en.wikipedia.org/w/index.php?title=Cerro_Rico&oldid=911606832.

[31] R, Alberto Crespo. *Fragmentos de la patria: doce estudios sobre la historia de Bolivia*. Plural editores, 2010.

[32] References are found on website *(general background information)*: "Huancavelica." In *Wikipedia*, May 12, 2019. https://en.wikipedia.org/w/index.php?title=Huancavelica&oldid=896705582.

[33] GUILLERMO LOHMANN VILLENA. "LAS MINAS DE HUANCAVELICA EN LOS SIGLOS XVI Y XVII," Sevilla 1949. https://www.google.com/url?sa=t&rct=j&q=&esrc=s&source=web&cd=13&cad=rja&uact=8&ved=2ahUKEwiCnYLU7oDlAhXEsJ4KHU7sAH0QFjAMegQIARAC&url=http%3A%2F%2Fdigital.csic.es%2Fbitstream%2F10261%2F164038%2F1%2FLas%2520minas%2520de%2520huancavelica%2520en%2520los%2520siglos%2520XVI%2520y%2520XVII.pdf&usg=AOvVaw26SIOpVu0bTsJDzHvoBkfm.

[34] Perú, Historia del. "Creación del Virreinato del Perú." Historia del Perú. Accessed October 9, 2019. https://historiaperuana.pe/periodo-colonial/virreinato/creacion-virreinato-peru/.

[35] References are found on website *(general background information):* "Piracy in the Caribbean." In *Wikipedia*, October 2, 2019. https://en.wikipedia.org/w/index.php?title=Piracy_in_the_Caribbean&oldid=919212964.

[36] Bernárdez, Torres. "Judge Sette-Camara, President of the Chamber Judges Sir Robert Jennings, President of the Court Oda, Vice-President of the Court," n.d., 63.

[37] "American Colonies - Honduras / Comayagua." Accessed October 6, 2019. https://www.historyfiles.co.uk/KingListsAmericas/CentralHonduras.htm.

[38] "ESCRIBANIA,1186 - Sentencias Del Consejo de Indias." PARES. Accessed October 9, 2019. http://pares.mcu.es:80/ParesBusquedas20/catalogo/description/87422.

[39] References are found on website *(general background information):* "History of Honduras." In *Wikipedia*, September 30, 2019. https://en.wikipedia.org/w/index.php?title=History_of_Honduras&oldid=918748371.

[40] Ancestry.com. "Alonso Lobato in the Bolivia, Select Baptisms, 1560-1938," Original data: Bolivia, Baptisms, -1938. Salt Lake City, Utah: FamilySearch, 2013 1560.

[41] References are found on website *(general background information):* "War of the Vicuñas and Basques." In *Wikipedia*, August 3, 2019. https://en.wikipedia.org/w/index.php?title=War_of_the_Vicu%C3%B1as_and_Basques&oldid=909162232.

[42] Cook, Noble David, and Alexandra Parma Cook. *People of the Volcano: Andean Counterpoint in the Colca Valley of Peru*. Duke University Press, 2007.

[43] Robins, Nicholas A., and Nicole A. Hagan. "Mercury Production and Use in Colonial Andean Silver Production: Emissions and Health Implications." *Environmental Health Perspectives* 120, no. 5 (May 2012): 627–31. https://doi.org/10.1289/ehp.1104192.

[44] "Genealogy, Family Trees and Family History Records Online - Ancestry®." Accessed October 10, 2019. https://www.ancestry.com/.

[45] PARES. "ESCRIBANIA,592B - COMISIONES GOBERNACION DE CARTAGENA." Accessed October 10, 2019. http://pares.mcu.es:80/ParesBusquedas20/catalogo/description/86469.

[46] Jaime Holcombe and awarded to Nuestros Ranchos por Don Guillermo Tovar de Teresa. "Revisar Notarías | Nuestros Ranchos." Accessed September 20, 2019. http://www.nuestrosranchos.com/es/notary/view/record/915.

[47] Rick Hendricks, Ph. D. "HERENCIA." In *LOBATO FAMILY ORIGINS IN SOMBRERETE, MEXICO*, 2nd ed. Vol. 2. Hispanic Genealogical Research **Center** of New Mexico, 1994.

[48] "A Forgotten Kingdom: The Spanish Frontier in Colorado and New Mexico, 1540-1821 (Chapter 1)." Accessed October 21, 2019. https://www.nps.gov/parkhistory/online_books/blm/ut/29/chap1.htm.

[49] Vargas, Diego de, John L. Kessell, Rick Hendricks, and Meredith D. Dodge. *Blood on the Boulders: The Journals of Don Diego de Vargas, New Mexico, 1694-97*. UNM Press, 1998.

[50] "Early Settlers of Santa Cruz de La Cañada 1695-1715 J A Esquibel 2015.Pdf." Accessed October 25, 2019. https://docs.google.com/viewer?a=v&pid=sites&srcid=ZGVmYXVsdGRvbWFpbnxiZXlvbmRvcmlnaW5zb2ZubWZhbWlsaWVzfGd4OjEzYTMxMGVhM2EyMzJlOTM.

[51] Vargas, Diego de, and John L. Kessell. *A Settling of Accounts: The Journals of Don Diego de Vargas, New Mexico, 1700-1704*. UNM Press, 2002.

[52] Twitchell, Ralph Emerson. *The Spanish Archives of New Mexico: Comp. and Chronologically Arranged with Historical, Genealogical, Geographical, and Other Annotations, by Authority of the State of New Mexico*. Torch Press, 1914.

[53] Nasonmc. "Nason McCormick: Land Grants." *Nason McCormick* (blog), October 18, 2015. http://nasonmcormic.blogspot.com/2015/10/land-grants.html.

[54] Vargas, Diego de, John L. Kessell, Rick Hendricks, and Meredith D. Dodge. *Blood on the Boulders: The Journals of Don Diego de Vargas, New Mexico, 1694-97*. UNM Press, 1998.

[55] Elmer Martinez. *LOBATO ORIGINALES EXPANOLES, Who Referenced Enciclopedia Ilustrada Universal, Madrid, Garcia Carraffa, Enciclopedia Heraldica, Madrid*. Spanish History Publications, n.d.

[56] Vargas, Diego de. *That Disturbances Cease: The Journals of Don Diego de Vargas, New Mexico, 1697-1700*. UNM Press, 2000.

[57] Chávez, Fray Angélico. *Origins of New Mexico Families: A Genealogy of the Spanish Colonial Period*. UNM Press, 2012.

[58] Virginia Langham Olmsted, C.G. "Spanish and Mexican Censuses of New Mexico 1750 to 1830," n.d.

[59] Chávez, Fray Angélico. *Origins of New Mexico Families: A Genealogy of the Spanish Colonial Period*. UNM Press, 2012.

[60] Poling-Kempes, Lesley. *Valley of Shining Stone: The Story of Abiquiu*. University of Arizona Press, 1997.

[61] Sánchez, Juan, Rita Padilla-Gutiérrez, Macario Griego, and Leonard Martínez. "Selections from J.J. Bowden's 'Private Land Claims in the Southwest,'" n.d., 189.

[62] Pike, David. *Roadside New Mexico: A Guide to Historic Markers*. UNM Press, 2004.

[63] Virginia Langham Olmsted, C.G. "Spanish and Mexican Censuses of New Mexico 1750 to 1830," n.d.

[64] Granville W and NC Hough. "SPAIN'S NEW MEXICO PATRIOUS IN ITS 1779-1783 WAR WITH ENGLAND DURING THE AMERICAN REVOLUTION, PART 4 OF SPANISH BORDERLANDS STUDIES," 1999. http://www.somosprimos.com/hough/newmex.pdf.

[65] Chavez, Angelico. "New Mexico Roots Ltd : A Demographic Perspective from Genealogical, Historical and Geographic Data Found in the Diligencias Matrimoniales or Pre-Nuptial Investigations (1678-1869) of the Archives of the Archdiocese of Santa Fe : Multiple Data Extracted and Here Edited in a Uniform Presentation by

Years and Family Surnames." *CSWR Reference Tools* 5 (January 1, 1983). https://digitalrepository.unm.edu/cswr_reference/5.

[66] FamilySearch. "Christobal Lobato in Entry for Maria De La Luz Lobato, 'New Mexico Births and Christenings, 1726-1918.'" Accessed November 5, 2019. /ark:/61903/1:1:FDNQ-TLQ.

[67] Twitchell, Ralph Emerson. *The Spanish Archives of New Mexico: Comp. and Chronologically Arranged with Historical, Genealogical, Geographical, and Other Annotations, by Authority of the State of New Mexico*. Torch Press, 1914.

[68] The Gorge Project. "Research (Embudo)," February 6, 2015. https://projectgorge.wordpress.com/our-results-2/research-embudo/.

[69] Karen Mitchell. "Bapsa." Accessed November 5, 2019. http://www.kmitch.com/Taos/bapsl.html.

[70] "Taos Valley Settlers." Accessed October 31, 2019. https://nmahgp.genealogyvillage.com/AllFamilyHistory/fhtaos_settlers.htm.

[71] "Lovato, Christobal. Case against Christobal Lovato and Others for Illegal Trade with Yutas. | UAiR." Accessed November 11, 2019. http://uair.library.arizona.edu/item/222370.

[71] FamilySearch. "Christobal Lobato in Entry for Juan Isidro Lobato and Salasar, 'New Mexico Marriages, 1751-1918.'" Accessed November 5, 2019. /ark:/61903/1:1:FDPW-3KZ.

[72] Herhahn, Cynthia L., and Ann F. Ramenofsky. *Exploring Cause and Explanation: Historical Ecology, Demography, and Movement in the American Southwest*. University Press of Colorado, 2016.

[73] Center for Land Grant Studies. 2008 1979. https://www.southwestbooks.org/sangredecristo.htm.

[74] FamilySearch. "Jose Francisco Lovato, 'New Mexico Marriages, 1751-1918.'" Accessed November 13, 2019. /ark:/61903/1:1:FDPG-Y2G.

[75] FamilySearch. "Jose Francisco Lovato in Entry for Jose Francisco Lovato, 'New Mexico Births and Christenings, 1726-1918.'" Accessed November 13, 2019. /ark:/61903/1:1:FDNW-LV1.

[76] Fold3. "Page 2 Civil War Soldiers - Union - NM." Accessed November 13, 2019. http://www.fold3.com:9292/image/265952519.

[77] FamilySearch. "Presentacion Lobato in Household of Jose F Labato, 'United States Census, 1910.'" Accessed November 13, 2019. /ark:/61903/1:1:MKW5-M9P.

[78] FamilySearch. "Presentacion Lobato, 'United States Census, 1940.'" Accessed November 13, 2019. /ark:/61903/1:1:VR67-XMJ.

Research Notes

Only a few people with the surname Lobato immigrated to America before the 1600s. [1] I have located documentation for each one of them in order to determine their fate. This process led me to my first ancestor, Alonso Lobato who immigrated to the West Indies. He was one of the first Spaniards in Panama, Peru, and Upper Peru (Bolivia) that had descendants that immigrated to Mexico, New Mexico, and Colorado. The men that survived with the Lobato name in this area have descended from him, because there is no other record of any other person with the Lobato surname except for a soldier who arrived later with Hernan Cortes from Mexico. This Soldier had one son before he died in battle. His son became a Priest with no heirs.

Investigation of Immigrants to America (1500-1600): (starting with oldest Immigrant)

1. Alonso Lobato - 1512   Arrival Place: West Indies (Hispanola)

    Alonso Lobato was listed as one of the Palermos from Palos de la Frontera that traveled to Santo Domingo in 1512 and then to Darien (Panama) in 1522. [2] He then joined the Francisco Pizarro expedition to Panama and Chili. [3] Alonso Lobato also joined the Francisco Pizarro expedition to conquer Peru and was rewarded with land in Quito in 1537. [4] Alonso Lobato survived with heirs.

2. Cristobal Lobato – 1519   Arrival Place: Cuba

    Cristobal Lobato was listed as one of the Palermos from Palos de la Frontera that traveled to Cuba in 1519 then to Mexico in 1520. [2] Cristobal Lobato joined the Pánfilo de Narváez expedition to Cuba then joined the Hernan Cortes expedition to conquer Mexico in 1520. [5] *He participated in the conquest of Colima and Michoacán, but no record of him has been located after those conquests. A Juan Lobato traveled with Hernan Cortes to Panama in later years who had only one heir who became a priest with no heirs. [6] The timeline and location determined that they were descendants of Cristobal Lobato.*

3. Pedro Lobato – 1528   Arrival Place: America

    Pedro Lobato joined the Hernando and Juan Pizarro's expedition to Cuzco in Peru where he was killed in the battle of las Salinas in 1538. [7] This battle occurred because Hernando and Juan Pizarro confronted a soldier, Diego de Almagro, who took Cuzco from them because he was upset that Francisco Pizarro did not give him credit for discovering Peru. [8]

4. Andres Lobato – 1535   Arrival Place: Rio de la Plata (South America)

    Andres Lobato was one of the first settlers in the territories of the Rio de la Plata and was present in the first foundation of Buenos Aires. He was recruited from Moron de la Frontera by Juan Osorio before he was killed as a traitor. [9] All those recruited by Osorio were kept in Buenos Aires to work where they were needed. Andres Lobato was added to a list by the Inquisition as being a Jewish Convert. [10] *There is no record of him traveling to America.*

5. Alvaro Lobato – 1535   Arrival Place: Nombre de Dios, Panama

Alvaro Lobato joined the expeditions of Diego de Almagro in Panama. [11] The men who joined Almagro participated in his conquest of Chili and later were killed or imprisoned when they battled Francisco Pizarro and his brothers in the battle of Salinas in 1538 where Almagro was defeated. [12] *There is no further record of Alvaro Lobato after the battle.*

6. Juan Lobato – 1535   Arrival Place: Rio de la Plata

Juan Lobato was the son of Hernando Dominguez Lobato who traveled with his father to Río de La Plata on July 28th, 1535, in the expedition of Pedro de Mendoza. [13] *There was no record of Juan Lobato traveling to America.*

7. Hernando Dominguez Lobato   Arrival Place: Rio de la Plata
    -1535
Hernando Dominguez Lobato and his son, Juan Lobato joined the Pedro de Mendoza expedition in 1535 to Rio de la Plata. The expedition arrived in Rio de la Plata in 1536 and founded Buenos Aires. Conquistadores on this expedition either returned to Spain or remained in Buenos Aires as settlers. [14] Hernando Lobato was still present in Rio de la Plata in 1576 when he petitioned for the freedom of an Indian. [15] *There is no record of him traveling to America.*

8. Fernan Dominguez Lobato   Arrival Place: Rio de la Plata
    -1535
Fernan Lobato was one of the first settlers in the territories of the Rio de la Plata and was present in the first foundation of Buenos Aires that was added to a list by the Inquisition as being a Jewish Convert who stayed as a settler instead of returning to Spain. [16] *There is no record of him traveling to America.*

9. Pedro Lobato – 1566   Arrival Place: New Spain

Pedro Lobato del Canto is the son of Francisco Lobato and a merchant of books from Medina del Campo, Spain. [17] He was a merchant of books in Mexico in 1577. [18] He applied for a license to fish for perils in Mexico in 1586 [19] and for another one to fish for perils in California in 1587. [20] He was transported back to Spain when he died in Colima, Mexico 1595 and left no will to his heirs. [21] *Pedro Lobato never left the Cuzco area, and his wife and heirs were recorded as being in Spain with no record of them traveling to America.*

10. Luis Lobato – 1581   Arrival Place: New Spain

Luis Lobato traveled with his guardian Juan Perez Pocasangre to New Spain. [22] He is the son of Maria Gabriel Lobato and Cristiano de Amberes, a famous painter. [23] *There is no further record of Luis Lobato in Mexico.*

References:

[1] *Duplicates and persons who migrated in the 1800s were crossed out.*

ancestry

All U.S. and Canada, Passenger and Immigration Lists Index, 1500s-1900s results for Lobato

Edit Search | New Search

Results 1–13 of 13

View Record	Name	Birth Year	Arrival Date	Arrival Place
View Record	Pedro Lobato		1566	New Spain
View Record	Francisco Lobato		1578	New Spain
View Record	Luis Lobato		1581	New Spain
View Record	Andres Lobato		1535	Rio de la Plata
~~View Record~~	~~Andres Lobato~~		~~1535~~	~~Rio de la Plata~~
View Record	Alonso Lobato		1512	West Indies
~~View Record~~	~~Fermin Lobato Alvarez~~		~~1571~~	~~Puerto Rico~~
View Record	Cristobal Lobato		1519	Cuba
View Record	Alvaro Lobato		1535	Nombre de Dios, Panama
View Record	Pedro Lobato		1528	America
View Record	Juan Lobato		1535	Rio de la Plata
View Record	Alvaro Lobato		1535	Nombre de Dios, Panama
~~View Record~~	~~Bto Fernandez Lobato~~	~~abt 1818~~	~~1854~~	~~New Orleans, Louisiana~~

1–13 of 13

Per page 20

All Categories

> Immigration & Travel

> Passenger Lists

U.S. and Canada, Passenger and Immigration Lists Index, 1500s-1900s

Updated annually, this database is an index to passengers who arrived in United States and Canadian ports from the 1500s through the 1900s. It contains listings of approximately 4,838,000...

Learn more about this database...

Shortcut Keys ▼

   New search

[2] LA EMIGRACION PALERMA A AMERICA, Julio IZQUIERDO LABRADO, Palos de la Frontera

http://rabida.uhu.es/dspace/bitstream/handle/10272/2894/b15126249.pdf?sequence=1 sub references: (1) BOWMAN, Boyd: Indice biogeográfico de 40.000 pobladores españoles de Indias. 2 tomos. Ed. Caro y Cuervo. Bogotá. 1964. (2) GOULD, Alicia E.: Nueva lista documentada de los tripulantes de Colón en 1492. «Boletín de la Real Academia de la Historia». Vol. LXXXVIII, págs. 721-789. Madrid, 1926. (3) MORALES PADRON, Francisco: Historia del Descubrimiento y Conquista de América. Editora Nacional. Madrid, 1983.

[3] Colección de Documentos inéditos para la historia de Chile: desde el Viaje de Magallanes hasta la Batalla de Maipo : 1518-1818 /Colectados y publicados por J. T. Medina. vol.IV
https://archive.org/details/raha_103067/page/n19

[4] Ducasse, Javier Ortiz de la Tabla. *Los encomenderos de Quito, 1534-1660: origen y evolución de una elite colonial*. Editorial CSIC - CSIC Press, 1993.

[5] Biblioteca Virtual, Miguel de Cervantes, **Carta del ejército de Cortés al emperador**
http://www.cervantesvirtual.com/obra-visor/coleccion-de-documentos-para-la-historia-de-mexico-version-actualizada--0/html/21bcd5af-6c6c-4b27-a9a5-5edf8315e835_25.html

[6] Real Academia de la Historia, Segundo Moreno Yáñez, F. González Suárez, *Historia General de la República del Ecuador,* Quito, CCE, 1969-1970; J. M. Vargas
http://dbe.rah.es/biografias/24813/diego-lobato-de-sosa-yarucpalla

[7] TEMAS DE HISTORIA Y ACTUALIDAD, Blog by Esteban Mira Caballos,
http://estebanmiracaballos.blogia.com/2017/031402-la-hueste-de-francisco-pizarro-todos-los-nombres-i-.php

[8] Colección de documentos inéditos para la historia de Chile ..., Volumes 5-6

https://books.google.com/books?id=XJA_CBD_dPMC&pg=RA1-PA342&lpg=RA1-PA342&dq=pedro+lobato+de+la+pena&source=bl&ots=85F234edXt&sig=oTmT9V48bqFBFkel8CFcknmx5rk&hl=en&sa=X&ved=0ahUKEwi4q_i-l77QAhXExFQKHUAXBk0Q6AEILDAF#v=onepage&q=pedro%20lobato%20de%20la%20pena&f=false

[9]**Revista de Historia bonaerense, Oct. 1988, MORÓN DESDE EL OTRO LADO DEL Mar, Javier Manchado Munox. Lic. En Geografia e Historia. Moron de la Frontera, Espana**
https://historiamoron.files.wordpress.com/2016/08/18-rhb-trabajadores.pdf

[10] BUENOS AIRES, CIUDAD CONVERSA, LA HEGEMONÍA CRIPTOJUDÍA EN EL PLATA DURANTE LA ÉPOCA HISPÁNICA, Federico Rivanera Caries
https://archive.org/details/BuenosAiresCiudadConversaPdf/page/n1

[11]Colección de documentos inéditos para la historia de Chile desde el viaje de Magallanes hasta la batalla de Maipo, 1518-1818 **https://archive.org/details/coleccindedocu05medi/page/n8**

[12] Diego de Almagro, Encyclopaedia Britannica, **PUBLISHER:** Encyclopaedia Britannica, Inc. **DATE PUBLISHED:** 01 January 2019 **ACCESS DATE:** September 04, 2019
URL: https://www.britannica.com/biography/Diego-de-Almagro

[13]Conquistadores Apellidos Españoles De Extremadura A Indias En Los Siglos Xv Y Xvi, Blog de Mayorga
http://mayorga-gen.blogspot.com/2006/10/d-conquistadores-apellidos-espaoles-de.html

[14] **Pedro de Mendoza, Encyclopedia Britannica, Inc. 19 June 2019**
https://www.britannica.com/biography/Pedro-de-Mendoza

[15]**Gorbieno de Espana, Ministerio de Cultura y Deporte,** Autos fiscales. Charcas, ES.41091.AGI/24//JUSTICIA,1133
http://pares.mcu.es/ParesBusquedas20/catalogo/description/93352

[16]BUENOS AIRES, CIUDAD CONVERSA, LA HEGEMONÍA CRIPTOJUDÍA EN EL PLATA DURANTE LA ÉPOCA HISPÁNICA, Federico Rivanera Caries
https://archive.org/details/BuenosAiresCiudadConversaPdf/page/n1

[17]La imprenta en Medina del Campo By Perez Pastor, Cristobal, d. 1908

https://archive.org/details/laimprentaenmed01pastgoog/page/n12

[18]Cuadernos Hispanoamericanos
http://bibliotecadigital.aecid.es/bibliodig/i18n/catalogo_imagenes/imagen.cmd?path=1005738&posicion=40&registrardownload=1

[19]© **Ministry of Culture and Sports - Spanish Government,** Consejo de Indias (España) - Producto
http://pares.mcu.es/ParesBusquedas20/catalogo/description/12733861

[20]© **Ministry of Culture and Sports - Spanish Government,** Consejo de Indias (España) - Producto
http://pares.mcu.es/ParesBusquedas20/catalogo/description/12692166

[21]© **Ministry of Culture and Sports - Spanish Government,** Consejo de Indias (España) - Producto
http://pares.mcu.es/ParesBusquedas20/catalogo/description/94869

[22]Pasajeros a Indias 1578-1585, Publicado el 5 octubre, 2018 por antepasadosblog
https://antepasadosblog.wordpress.com/2018/10/05/pasajeros-a-indias-1578-1585/

[23]CRISTIANO DE AMBERES, PAINTER OF PHILIP II. DOCUMENTARY FACTS, JOSÉ LUIS CANO DE GARDOQUI GARCÍA Universidad de Valladolid https://uvadoc.uva.es/bitstream/handle/10324/9018/BSAAArte-2011-77-CristianodeAmberes.pdf;jsessionid=43F813CA99FBA59BA1C42A3CB8944AD1?sequence=1

Additional Notes:

Lobato name suspected of being Jewish (Added to Inquisition Lists)

During the Inquisition in Spain and Portugal, Jews were forced to convert to Catholicism (Conversos) or they would have to leave. Many joined the expeditions to America until lists were created of the suspected Jewish Converts. A list known as "Huellas" was created in Spain that identified surnames of those who were of a possible Jewish origin based on the meaning of their family name and family members who openly declared themselves Jews. The name Lobato was included on this list. [1]

Also, a list of Jewish Hispanics was created in Ecuador that included patronymic names or names belonging to the father. This list of Spanish-Hebrew patronymics was extracted from various sources ranging from the lists of the Marranos judged and burned by the Inquisition to the oral testimony of several people who know and remember the Spanish-Hebrew ancestor of their families. The Lobato name was included in this list. [2]

A list was also created in Buenos Aries of suspected and confessed Jews. Very few Lobato men traveled out of Spain in the early 1500s to the Indies. Andres Lobato and Hernan Dominguez Lobato, who traveled to the Indies were both included on this list. [3]

When Spain expelled the Jews, many went to Portugal. During the 1600s, Spain passed a law that no more Portuguese were to be admitted into Mexico. Recent Portuguese arrivals were to be carefully questioned and their papers and letters investigated. Portuguese ships were, from then on, prohibited from Mexican as from other Spanish-American ports. [4]

[1]El origen de los apellidos Núñez, Lobato, Morón y Ábalos (de Ábalos) https://www.radiosefarad.com/el-origen-de-los-apellidos-nunez-lobato-moron-y-abalos-de-abalos/

[2]La Herencia Sefardita En La Provincia De Loja, Ricardo Ordonez Chiriboga http://sefaradaragon.org/documentos/PDF/Sefarditas%20en%20Loja.pdf

[34BUENOS AIRES, CIUDAD CONVERSA, LA HEGEMONÍA CRIPTOJUDÍA EN EL PLATA DURANTE LA ÉPOCA HISPÁNICA, Federico Rivanera Caries https://archive.org/stream/BuenosAiresCiudadConversaPdf/buenos%20aires%20ciudad%20conversa%20pdf_djvu.txt

[4]THE PORTUGUESE IN SEVENTEENTH-CENTURY MEXICO, By J. I.Israel https://www.degruyter.com/downloadpdf/j/jbla.1974.11.issue-1/jbla-1974-0104/jbla-1974-0104.pdf

www.ingramcontent.com/pod-product-compliance
Lightning Source LLC
Chambersburg PA
CBHW082055090726
47909CB00010B/3045